RARELY KNOWN

RARELY

KNOWN

FACTS ENIGMAS CURIOSITIES

SASHA POGREBINSKY

ELEMENT PRESS • NEW YORK

PUBLISHED BY ELEMENT PRESS
elementpress.org • *rarelyknown.org* • *pogrebinsky.info*

Special thanks to W.W. Norton & Company for permission to publish a selection from Jan Banderon's work *Buried Alive: The Terrifying History of Our Most Primal Fear.*

Pogrebinsky, Sasha A.
Rarely known: facts, enigmas, curiosities / Pogrebinsky, Alexander.

ISBN-13: 978-0-615-42800-0
ISBN-10: 0-6154-2800-2

Element Press Cataloging Number
EP-NF-0001

Element Press publishes books of general interest, art, history, literary translations, and fiction. Our mission is to produce high quality books by innovative writers and artists. *For more intriguing and illuminating facts see the Rarely Known website at www.rarelyknown.org*

Cover image is a detail of Alexander Pogrebinsky's (1951-) oil painting *Where Is The Truth?* (1995) of Pontius Pilate debating Jesus Christ's fate. For more information on the artist and the painting visit www.pogrebinsky.com

For my parents
Lena and Alexander Pogrebinsky

CONTENTS

INTRODUCTION

Rarely Known is a collection of useful bits of information which you may not come across in your daily business. The small book touches upon philosophy, religion, music, literature, nature, medicine, science, and other aspects of human endeavor – all randomly placed into a neat little book for your intellectual fulfillment.

Most of the information contained came while I was a graduate student at New York University, combing through countless books, stumbling upon curious thoughts and characters often residing within the hidden and cramped walls of a footnote. I would mark their names down in a notebook as an archeologist might a fragment of clay amongst a greater excavation, for more than not they were unrelated to the research I was conducting at the time. They remained in the notebook, confined to a life of patience and silence, just as they were confined years prior in those footnotes. But today I bring them to you, where they finally belong, onto the big pages, where they can present themselves as important elements of a rarely known yet splendidly curious cosmology.

I believe this book will serve the purposes of both entertaining and enlightening. I did not want to collect a book of useless factoids, as they are often called, that impress people with the speeds of crocodiles and the sort, rather a book of information which one would simply not have the time to bother looking up, and which most certainly would spark a curiosity towards something. It is a small collection of interesting information, dealing with religion, history, science, myth, and the arts. It is a thinking man's companion for a single day's voyage, a text to stimulate the bored, overworked, and overwhelmed.

Surely not everything contained within is "rarely known." To some all of the information could be in fact well known, yet I feel for the majority of us, busy with the nonsensical business of death and taxes, we rarely have the chance to learn about the Yanomani, sin-eaters, crazed dancers, and mysterious manuscripts.

In attempting to keep this work short, I'll make my introduction a place for acknowledgments as well. The only ones on the list are my family, who despite having an absurdly busy life, found time to read and reread this little manuscript. I would like to thank my father Alexander, and mother Lena, without your knowledge, motivation, and inspiration this book would never have been possible. Also my sister Natasha, whose busy career as a chef and professor did not prevent her assisting me in the creation of this little book of curiosities.

Sasha Pogrebinsky
New York City, 2014

DANCING MADNESS

Dancing manias are a social phenomenon of people suddenly joining dancing crazes which often involve hundreds or thousands and can last for several days or weeks. These manias were predominant in fourteenth and seventeenth century Europe and some scholars have traced these manias as far back as 1017 to a Saxon town of Kolbigk where people danced maniacally in a graveyard.

Others have pointed to the 1020s when eighteen peasants disturbed a Christmas Eve service by dancing around a church in Bernburg, Germany. According to German scribes in 1247 over one-hundred children danced through the town of Erfurt, Germany. German chronicles write of how the children danced out of the town into the neighboring village where from exhaustion many had fallen down by the village's gates, some of them dying from exhaustion, the others that had survived were crippled for the rest of their lives with terrible tremors.

In 1278 close to two-hundred people danced on a bridge over the Moselle River, having danced so long that the bridge collapsed killing all those afflicted with the madness.

Perhaps the most fascinating and well documented episode of dancing madness took place in the French town of Strasbourg in the summer of 1518 when a certain Frau Troffea started dancing in the streets. The woman danced the whole week, and within that week close to one-hundred people joined her. By the end of the month over four-hundred people were dancing without rest on the streets of Strasbourg.

Physicians informed the concerned authorities that the only cure for the seemingly unexplainable dance craze was more dancing.[1] Soon guildhalls were set up and professional musicians and dancers were hired to help the afflicted dance-out their madness. Some who had danced without rest or had taken a break began to suffer from heart attacks and exhaustion and some died.

By the end of August those who kept dancing were loaded into wagons and sent off to a healing shrine. There are several historical explanations for this strange mass dancing phenomenon. Some propose that the dancers had consumed ergot, a psychotropic mold that grows on rye and causes hallucinations. Others suppose that the dancing was an act of a cult or sect, while historian John Waller argues that it was caused by a mass psychogenic illness as a result of experiencing the famines of previous years.

---

[1] It was commonly believed that more music and dancing would often cure this form of madness.

The dancing mania was dubbed *chorea lasciva* by the sixteenth-century occultist Paracelsus in his 1532 mystical treatise *Diseases that Rob Men of Their Reason* which he wrote after spending some time in Strasbourg. Later it was called St. John's Dance because it was believe that only St. John could alleviate the madness, and some have suggested that it was called St. John's Dance due to a bizarre cult of St. John, for dancers often flocked to chapels in his honor, or began their dancing madness on his day. Later the madness was associated with another saint, that of St. Vitus for similar mystical reasoning.

See: Waller, John. *A Time to Dance a Time to Die*. Manchester, UK: Icon Books, 2008.

THE AMBER ROOM

The Amber Room is a room in the Catherine Palace at Tsarskoye Selo near St. Petersburg, Russia. It is a chamber decorated completely out of amber panels with gold leaf. Because of its breathtaking beauty and complexity it was often called the Eighth Wonder of the World.

It was originally built between 1701 and 1709 by German and Russian craftsmen and installed at the Charlottenburg Palace, the home of Freidrich I of Prussia. In 1716 Peter I of Russia visited Freidrich I, and after being so impressed with the Amber Room, Freidrich presented Peter with it as an act of generosity, cementing a Prussian-Russian alliance.

In 1755 Czarina Elizabeth of Russia had the room moved and installed at the Winter Palace and later into the Catherine Palace.

During World War II Adolf Hitler allowed the German military to move culturally significant possessions from occupied territories into Germany. Fearing that the room would be stolen from Leningrad, Soviet curators attempted to move the room, but having difficulty and since the amber was so delicate, the only solution was to conceal it and safeguard it in whatever way possible. A handful of curators decided to conceal the room by covering the amber with layers of cloth and padding in an attempt to deceive the Nazi's.

During the Nazi invasion and siege of Leningrad (originally called St. Petersburg) the room was stripped of its amber within 36 hours by German soldiers and moved to Konigsberg Castle for storage. When the war had moved against the Germans in 1945 the castle was bombed by the Royal Air Force; however rumors abounded that the room had already been moved to Weimer by the Germans aboard the *Wilhelm Gustoff* flagship. The original room was never to be seen again. A whole industry of salvage experts has emerged who continually scour the catacombs beneath the German city of Weimer, and divers often explore the wrecked flagship.

In 1979 the Soviets began a painstaking reconstruction of the Amber Room, completing it in 2003. In 1999 a German company helped construct the replica with a gift of 3.3 million dollars.

See: Clark, Cathy, and Adrian Levy. *The Amber Room: the fate of the world's greatest lost treasure*. New York: Walker & Co., 2004.

PLEASURE MANUALS

Pleasure manuals, or sex-manuals, are books which give advice and information on the performance of sexual acts with other human beings, as well as advice on child birth and how to maintain a healthy sexual lifestyle.

The earliest sex manuals are from Asia, and the Chinese *Handbooks of Sex,* which dates to the third-century BC written by the legendary "Yellow Emperor" Huang Di, is considered the oldest in the world. Historian R.H. van Gulik describes the books:

"The conjugal sexual relations referred to in these texts must be considered against the background of the polygamic family system, in which a middle-class householder had three or four, upper middle class persons six to twelve, and members of the nobility, great generals and princes thirty or more wives and concubines. For instance, the repeated advice of the handbooks that a man should copulate with a number of different women on the same night – in a monogamic society an exhortation to gross license – in ancient China falls entirely within the scope of marital sex relations."[1]

One of the oldest Indian manuals, dating between the fourth and sixth century AD, is the *Kama Sutra* by Mallanaga Vatsyayana.[2] The work is organized into seven parts. The first part is an introduction; the second deals with several types of stimulations and positions; the third with marriage, obtaining women, and "dealing with" women; the fourth with the role and conduct of a wife; the fifth deals with how men and woman behave together; the sixth part deals with relationships with a former lover, and related topics; the seventh and final part deals with improving physical attractions and other sections.

The first English translation appeared in 1883 in private print by Sir Richard Francis Burton, who provided the footnotes and the introduction to an edition mostly put together by Bhagvanal Indraji, Foster Fitzgerald Arbuthnot, and Shivaram Parshuram Bhide.[3]

---

[2] *Kama* means "pleasure" and *sutra* is a Sanskrit word for a collection of aphorisms forming a manual, therefore a *pleasure manual.*

[3] Sir Richard Francis Burton (1821-1890) was an English polymath, an explorer, orientalist, linguist, poet, scholar, diplomat, occultist, and wide variety of other professions. Burton was fascinated by languages and human behavior. A restless explorer, he was amongst the first Europeans to explore Africa, searching for the source of the Nile,

The Perfumed Garden is a fifteenth-century Arabic sexual manual written by Muhammad ibn Muhammad al-Nafzawi. The text gives information on sexual techniques, sexual remedies, and explains the methods by which men and women may make themselves more appealing to the opposite sex. There is also a section on the interpretation of sexual dreams. Sections of *The Perfumed Garden* contain titles such as "On the Deceits and Treacheries of Women," "Of Things that Take Away the Bad Smell from the Armpit and Sexual Parts of Women and Contract the Latter," and "About Men Who Are to Be Held in Contempt."

Dr. David Reuben's 1969 manual *Everything You Always Wanted to Know About Sex (But Were Afraid to Ask)* was the first modern sexual manual to enter mainstream culture and become part of the so-called Sexual Revolution of the late 1960s and early 1970s. Alex Comfort's 1972 *The Joy of Sex* also become part of the mainstream, and received some controversy after its publication mostly due to religious groups opposing its inclusion in public libraries. Comfort's book maintains a

---

and later discovering Lake Tanganyika. Burton was the first European non-Muslim to go on the Haj. His pilgrimage to Mecca was conducted in various disguises, where he would paint his skin olive, wear native garb, and converse in fluent Arabic. Burton was the first to translate the full version of the *Arabian Nights* and introduced, and translated the sexual manuals *The Kama Sutra* and *The Perfumed Garden* into the English language. Burton spoke over 30 languages fluently. For more information see Edward Rice's 2001 biography *Captain Sir Richard Francis Burton.*

humorous and light-hearted attitude towards human sexuality.

See: Vatsyayana, Mallanaga. *Kamasutra (Oxford World's Classics)*. Reissue ed. New York: Oxford University Press, USA, 2009.

TREE OF TENERE

The Tree of Tenere, or "Abre du Ténéré," was a solitary acacia, once considered to be the most isolated tree on the planet which grew in the middle of the Ténéré Desert in Niger, being the only tree for about 250 miles in any direction. According to Alison Behnke, the tree was considered sacred by some.[II]

Largely due to its beauty and inspirational isolation the tree had acquired a legendary stature and became a destination of sorts for adventurers, explorers, and people traveling along the caravan route. It was reported that the tree sprouted green and yellow flowers. In 1939 Michel Lesourd, Commander of Central Service of Saharan Affairs, wrote of the tree:

"One must see the Tree to believe its existence. What is its secret? How can it still be living in spite of the multitudes of camels which trample at its sides. How at each azalai does not a lost camel eat its leaves and thorns?[4] Why don't the numerous Touareg leading the salt caravans cut its branches to make fires to brew their tea? The only answer is that the tree is taboo and considered as such by the caravaniers. There is a kind of superstition, a tribal order which is always respected. Each year the azalaigather round the Tree before facing the crossing of the Ténéré. The Acacia has become a living lighthouse; it is the first or the last landmark for the *Azalai* leaving Agadez for Bilma, or returning."[III]

In 1973 the tree was struck by an apparently drunk driver snapping its trunk. The tree died soon after the incident, and was later moved to Niamey's National Museum while a metallic monument was placed on the spot, marking its once isolated and legendary existence.

DIOGENES OF SINOPE

Diogenes of Sinope was a Greek philosopher of the Cynic school who is best known for his particular sense of humor, wit, and whose peculiar ascetic methods of espousing his theories have become legendary.

Originally a citizen of Sinope, he would later be banished for defacing the state currency. Afterwards, he travelled to

---

[4] The Azalai is a semi-annual salt caravan route practiced by the Tuareg, a nomadic group of people inhabiting the Sahara. It may also just mean the act of going on a caravan route.

Athens where he defied social norms by eating in the market-place and walking through the market at daytime with a lamp claiming that he was searching for an honest man – suggesting that no honest man resided in Athens. It was in Athens too that Diogenese famously lived in a wooden barrel near the market.[5]

Diogenes believed that man should not focus on the socially created norms of wealth, power, and standing, but rather on attaining happiness through a simple life, without too much care for health, cleanliness, and the opinions of others. He used his wit and humor to make his points, for example when Plato defined man as a "featherless biped" Diogenes brought him a plucked chicken saying "Behold – a man!"

Legends state that when Alexander the Great visited Corinth he exchanged a few words with the famous and controversial philosopher. When Alexander found Diogenese sitting in the sun enjoying the outdoors the King of Macedon asked the famous philosopher if there was anything he could do for him. "Please move out of my sunlight" was the philosopher's response.

---

[5] In Ancient Greece it was against the law to deface currency, though we do not know in exactly what way Diogenes defaced it, if he really did so. In most countries it is illegal to deface currency, much like it is illegal to deface other parts of state property or symbolism, such as a flag. In Ancient Greece the marketplace was revered, and it was considered taboo to eat and sleep there.

It is believed that Diogenese lived a long life, dying perhaps at ninety. His death, just as his life, has become legend. Some state that he died as a result of a dog bite, which is ironic because the word Cynic derives from the Greek *kynikos*, meaning "dog-like," supposedly because of their open rejection of conventional manners. After his death a memorial was erected with a statue of a dog.

See: Navia, Luis E.. *Diogenes of Sinope: the man in the tub*. Westport, Conn.: Greenwood Press, 1998.

COMMUNIST SYMBOLISM

The signs and symbolism of Communism are based upon the Marxist principles of class warfare, workers revolution, international solidarity, and the struggle for a classless society. Almost all Communist symbols are red, the color of the worker's movement and the blood of the workers. The most widely used symbol is the red star, which is a pentagram with the insides bled in.

The five points on the star represent the five fingers of the worker's hand, the five continents of the world, and/or the five classes of a socialist society – the workers, farmers, intellectuals, soldiers, and youth.

A widely recognized symbol of Communism is the red flag which originates in 1871 with the French Revolution. The most recognizable symbol however is that of the hammer and sickle. The hammer represents the workers and the sickle represents the farmers. It originates in Russia during the 1917 Revolution, but was not the official symbol until 1922.

Various other communist nations, parties, groups, and affiliations have adopted the Soviet symbol and have either used the original hammer and sickle design or modified it to their own preference. For example, the flag of the Worker's Party of Korea (today's North Korea) has a hammer, sickle, and a writing brush; the Communist Party of England uses a hammer and a dove but looks somewhat like a hammer and sickle.

STOWAWAY

Stowaways are people who travel in containers, luggage, boxes, or by hiding in any form of transport instead of being a passenger. Sometimes these people are referred to as "human mail."

The circumstances surrounding one becoming a stowaway vary but it is generally either voluntary attempts at fleeing the country a country from which travel is restricted or attempts at breaking into a country which does not accept people of a certain nationality. According to FAA spokesman Ian Gregor there have been 74 known stowaway attempts worldwide and only 14 of these individuals have survived.[IV]

The most recent case of a stowaway took place on June 9, 2010 when a 20-year old Romanian national stowed himself in the rear wheel cavity of a Boeing 747 owned by an Arab sheik traveling from Vienna to Britain's Heathrow airport. The man survived only because the plane flew at a low altitude to avoid stormy weather. The young man was allowed to remain in Britain.

CARRIER PIGEONS

Carrier pigeons are a domesticated pigeon, also known as homing pigeons, which have been trained to carry messages. Homing pigeons are unique in that they have an ability to fly long distances back to their nests, flying up to 50 miles per hour over 1,000 miles. Carrier pigeons were widely used during the nineteenth and twentieth-centuries, specifically for mail or to carry life-saving medicine to remote areas. The Racing Homer is a breed of pigeon bred specifically for racing, averaging 60 miles per hour in long distances and up to 110 miles per hour in shorter distances.

Pigeons have also been used as aerial photographers as early as 1903 by attaching a lightweight time-delayed miniature camera to their breast. Most advances in pigeon photography resulted from the work of German inventor Julius Neubronner who came up with the method of attaching camera's to pigeons. Pigeon photographers were widely used during World War I and even as late as World War II.

In the February 1930 report on carrier pigeons *Popular Mechanics* reported on perhaps the most well-known and heroic bird of the early twenty-first century:

". . .Then there was "The Mocker." A dark-red bird, of doubtful breeding, his best known feat took place early on the morning of September 12, 1918. With one eye destroyed by a shell splinter, this game fellow raced home in splendid time from the vicinity of Beaumont front, St. Mihiel sector, bearing a message of great importance. Not only did the information thus sent give the location of certain heavy enemy batteries, but it enabled the Yank artillery to silence the rival guns within twenty minutes."[V]

HOLODOMOR

The Holodomor, or "death by hunger," was a man-made famine that took the lives of eight to ten million Soviet Ukrainians between 1932 and 1933. It remains a poorly understood and controversial period in Soviet history, and is almost rarely known outside of Eastern Europe. And even though it took place over seventy years ago, scholars, journalists, and politicians continue to debate whether the famine was a general attack on the peasantry or genocide against the Ukrainian people.

Scholars and journalists who study the famine from an ethno-centric viewpoint argue that Stalin's fear of Ukrainian nationalism, Ukraine's strong peasant resistance, and the nationalist characteristics and elements within Ukrainian universities, intelligentsia, and the Communist Party of Ukraine led to the deliberate implementation of aggressive policies of forced collectivization[6] and *dekulakization*[7] which resulted in the starvation of millions of ethnic Ukrainians.

Large numbers of pro-Russian and Western scholars argue that the famine cannot be fully understood within national terms, but rather should be studied from a class-based ideological framework. This argument points to Stalin's phobia of the peasantry as a class-enemy, a class which had to be fully eradicated in order to create a socialist order composed of a conscious proletariat lead by a disciplined vanguard, the Party. They argue that in order for this revolution to take place the peasantry had to be forcibly industrialized and collectivized, despite any kind of opposition.

Though the peasantry supposedly played a fundamental part in Soviet society, it was the proletariat which was seen as

---

[6] *Forced collectivization* was the Soviet policy of forcing Soviet farmers into farm collectives, known as the *kolkhoz*.

[7] *Dekulakization* was the policy of purging the peasantry of wealthy, private-property minded peasants known as the *kulaks* (in Russian meaning *fist*).

the natural ally of a socialist state, and the peasantry, with its tendency towards private ownership of land, was its natural enemy. This argument would claim that it was simply a matter of unfortunate circumstances that ethnic Ukrainians composed over eight-percent of the peasantry of the USSR.

Whatever academics and politicians posit the fact remains that the Holodomor was the single worst tragedy for the Ukrainian people in the 20th century aside from the Chernobyl nuclear disaster.

Between 1932 and 1933, eight to ten million Ukrainians died from hunger due to excessive grain procurements. Young, fanatical, and poorly trained communists from the USSR's urban centers were sent by the thousands into Ukrainian villages to collect every drop of grain. When the grain procurements did not meet the unrealistic quotas, they began to take the food from the peasant's home. When the peasantry began starving and attempted to flee to seek food and work in the cities, the newly created internal passport system forced them to remain in their villages where famine was so rampant that some resorted to cannibalism.

The grain requisitions were so excessive that taking a single ear of grain became an offense punishable by death. The decree of August 7 1932, penned by Stalin and signed by Kalinin, Molotov, and Enukidze, commonly referred to as the Law of Spikelets, stated that anyone, caught hand-collecting the left-overs of grain were to be shot, including children.

These horrors took place while the USSR was exporting grain to Western Europe and cozying up to the British and the Americans in order to build better political and trade relations. And although Western powers were fully aware of the dire situation, financial and political interests superseded the millions of silent deaths in the Soviet countryside.

Despite the indifference of Western governments, Western scholars and Ukrainian émigré's worked diligently to raise awareness. In 1933 Ukrainians staged mass marches in major North American cities, protested outside consulates, sent letters to diplomats, and published detailed stories of starvation in Ukrainian and English-language newspapers, to little avail.

English-language reporters such as Gareth Jones and Malcolm Muggeridge wrote numerous articles in American and British papers about the dire situation, their works were met with disinterest in the West and complete denial in the East.

It was not until the 1950s, at the height of the Cold War, that the Holodomor began to receive serious attention. Fueled by anti-Communist interests and a well-organized Ukrainian émigré community in North America, awareness of Soviet atrocities and the unexplained decline of the Ukrainian population between 1932-33, as well as the case of the missing 1937 Soviet census, began to prompt interest in what has become known by some as the Ukrainian holocaust.

See: Conquest, Robert. *The harvest of sorrow: Soviet collectivization and the terror-famine*. New York: Oxford University Press, 1986.

SPACE WEATHER

Space weather refers to changing conditions within space in relation to radiation, charged particles, solar winds, magnetic fields, and other matter that exists in outer space. Space weather depends almost exclusively on the conditions of the Sun.

The Sun experiences storms called Solar Flares and Coronal Mass Ejections which release tremendous amounts of radiation and strong magnetic fields into space. These storms go into all areas of space, at times hitting planet Earth, affecting life on Earth in many ways. Space storms can damage satellites and knock out electricity. They can also create beautiful displays of light within our atmosphere known as auroras; the two most common auroras are the Aurora Borealis and Aurora Australis.

There have been several such storms that have affected our planet. The solar superstorm of September 1-2 1859 was the most powerful in recorded history, resulting in aurorae being seen all around the world. The aurorae were so bright that their glow awoke miners in the Rocky Mountains; some miners even began preparing breakfast thinking it was morning.

On September 1, Richard Carrington (1826-1875), an amateur British astronomer, observed the largest recorded solar flare, travelling to earth in only 18 hours and not the typical two or three days. The solar storm of 1859 is often cited as the Carrington Event.

The United States National Research Council writes:

"Dramatic displays had been seen five nights before as well, on the night of August 28/29 when . . . the whole celestial vault was glowing with streamers, crimson, yellow, and white, gathered into waving brilliant folds. In New York City, thousands gathered on sidewalks and rooftops to watch "the heavens . . . arrayed in a drapery more gorgeous than they have been for years." The aurora that New Yorkers witnessed that Sunday night, *The New York Times* assured its readers, "will be referred to hereafter among the events which occurred but once or twice in a lifetime."

"From August 28 through September 4, auroral displays of extraordinary brilliance were observed throughout North and South America, Europe, Asia, and Australia, and were seen as far south as Hawaii, the Caribbean, and Central America in the Northern Hemisphere and in the Southern Hemisphere as far north as Santiago, Chile. Even after daybreak, when the aurora was no longer visible, its presence continued to be felt through the effect of auroral currents."[VI]

See: Moldwin, Mark. *An Introduction to Space Weather*. New York: Cambridge University Press, 2008.

MARK OF THE BEAST: 666 or 616.

The "Mark of the Beast" is a Biblical concept found in the New Testament's Book of Revelation. Revelation 13:17-18 of the King James Version reads:

". . .no man might buy or sell, save he that had the mark, or the name of the beast, or the number of his name. Here is wisdom. Let him that hath understanding count the number of the beast: for it is the number of a man, and his number is six hundred threescore and six."

The Church Fathers have interpreted these statements as being prophetic, and therefore describing some sort of Antichrist that shall come about. Furthermore they have attempted to decipher the name of this coming Antichrist through the number.

The earliest recorded church historian and theologian to seriously deal with the mystical Antichrist was Irenaeus, the Gallic Bishop of Lugdunum writing between 180 and 190 AD.

Irenaeus was troubled by the fact that some manuscripts or writers gave the number as 616, but was sure that it was an error, as he had just shown to his satisfaction, that 666 was necessarily right, for the flood came in the 600th year of Noah and the image set up by Nebuchadnezzar was 60 cubits high and 6 cubits wide. He accordingly interpreted only the number 666.[VII] Irenaeus gave three names in Greek which if one takes the numerical values of the Greek letters and adds them comes up with the number 666.

Many scholars followed Irenaeus's tradition, because in this fashion many names could be found. For example Primasius found two names, Victorinus finds another three, and many others use this kind of mathematical approach to the Greek alphabet and to the leaders of the time period in an attempt to figure out who the Antichrist is. Surprisingly this system of searching for the Antichrist within the number 666 survived into the twentieth century, but this has been limited.

Most scholars search for past Church offenders and tyrants who could fit into this number and most have concluded that the most likely candidate is Emperor Nero whose name in Aramaic equals 666.

In 2005 a papyrus codex discovered by English papyrologist Arthur Surridge Hunt, called Papyrus 15, was decoded, which supposedly reveals that the mark of the beast is 616. [8]

Nevertheless debate continues as to what the actual number is and what it means – does it represent a past transgressor or a future one? There are many problems facing those who are attempting the deciphering process, certain names work only

---

[8] Papyrus 15, or P15, is a manuscript dating to the third century, containing 1 Corinthians 7:18-8:4, written in Greek, as of 2011 housed in the Egyptian Museum in Cairo.

under certain mathematical formulas and formulas of linguistics, and these formulas become ever more useless if these names are written in other languages prevalent in that day, for example if the Greek spelling of Nero Ceasar is transliterated into Hebrew it equals 666, if however this same method is applied to Latin it equals 616 and so forth.

CHIVALRIC AND MEDIEVAL VIRTUES

Chivalry often refers to a gentleman's code of conduct, especially his concern for the wellbeing of others, his courtesy before women, courage, and the honor of his family and name. The term originates from the French word *chevalier*, meaning "knight." Most chivalric orders were formed in the Middle Ages.

Though no specific code was written in stone it has been generally accepted that in order for a man to behave chivalrously he must possess the following virtues: Justice (fairness and equality), Strength (force and might), Courage (bravery), Mercy (pity and compassion), Prudence (intelligence and discretion), Temperance (restraint and moderation), Faith (belief and trust), Humility (modesty and meekness), Nobility (of noble blood), and Purity (freedom from contamination).

The influence of Christianity upon these virtues cannot be overlooked as Christianity fundamentally formed the social conventions and culture of medieval Europe. While the church was actively tolerant of war and violence in defense of its faith and institutions, it was nonetheless promoting peace and kindness towards fellow Christians and countrymen.

The *Pax Dei* and *Truega Dei* proclamations of the late 980s were attempts to pacify feudal society. The *Pax Dei* proclamation at the Synod of Charroux in 989 proclaimed anathema on those who robbed the poor, broke into churches, or attacked unarmed clergymen.

See: Barber, Richard, and Juliet Barker. *Tournaments: Jousts, Chivalry and Pageants in the Middle Ages*. New Ed ed. Rochester, NY: Boydell Press, 2000.

SKY BURIAL

A sky burial, or *jhator*, is the Tibetan ritual in which the human corpse is left in the open exposed to the elements and fed upon by vultures. Prior to the sky burial monks chant mantras around the body followed by a disassembling of the corpse. Sometimes the body is snapped and wrapped in cloth and left on a mountain for the vultures to tear apart the flesh. Once all flesh has been consumed monks may turn the bones into ash and feed it to other animals. The practice was forbidden by the People's Republic of China beginning in the late 1950s but since the 1980s it has been allowed. The religious purpose for the *jhator* is that it symbolizes the impermanence of life.

The *jhator* has similarities with the ancient Tower of Silence, or more correctly the *dakhma*, a Zoroastrian funerary tower on which the dead were disposed. Exposed to the sun and vultures, once the corpse had turned to bone they then fell to the bottom where they disintegrated.

The *dakhma* continues to be used today in limited form. It is a circular stone tower constructed upon a hill with an iron door that opens to the platform on which the bodies are disposed. The platform is made up of three circles, the largest being for the bodies of men, the middle being for the bodies of women, and the smallest being for the bodies of children. The remaining bones are later placed in a large deep hole at the center of the tower.[VIII]

See: Xue, Xinran. *Sky Burial: An Epic Love Story of Tibet*. New York: Anchor, 2006.

THUGGS

In today's culture one tends to hear the term *thug* referring to an urban subculture of drugs and gangs. This lifestyle is also known as *thug-life* – an existence which romanticizes the realities of dealing drugs, selling guns, and involvement in prostitution, as well as prison life. Many are unaware that the origins of the term *thug* are to be found in India where a cult of thieves, hooligans, and early-gangsters harassed colonial society in the seventeenth-century.

The cult was known as Thugee, named after its leader and mass-murderer Thug Behram, and began as a fraternity in the early thirteen-hundreds, over time turning into a complicated inner-society of professional robbers trained in the art of stealing and killing.[9]

Over the centuries "thuggery" became a large problem as foreign caravans became their target, and the loss of lives grew to a significant amount. The British authorities in India made it a priority to stamp out the cult. It is believed that the cult or its modern form is still in existence to this day.

VRIL

In 1871 English writer Edward Bulwer-Lytton published the cult novel *Vril: The Power of the Coming Race*. The novel told the story of a young traveler who makes his way into the underground world occupied by people who call themselves the Vril-ya. The Vril-ya possess and control a certain power, or energy, called the Vril. The Vril has the ability to heal and destroy, and the Vril-ya children are the most powerful, capable of destroying whole cities with their thoughts. Bulwer-

---

[9] Thug Behram was born sometime in the 1760s, and is believed to have murdered over 930 people by strangulating his victims with a *rumāl*, a kind of Hindi handkerchief. He is considered one of the most prolific killers in human history, some claiming that he had killed over 930 people in his lifetime. Behram was executed in 1840.

Lytton wrote that the Vril-ya were descendants of an ancient civilization which perished during a massive deluge in pre-history, alluding to Atlantis. The Vril-ya had a kind of wand, or staff, through which the Vril was channeled. Lytton writes:

"I have spoken so much of the Vril Staff that my reader may expect me to describe it. This I cannot do accurately, for I was never allowed to handle it for fear of some terrible accident occasioned by my ignorance of its use; and I have no doubt that it requires much skill and practice in the exercise of its various powers . . . Some were more potent to destroy, others to heal; much also depended on the calm and steadiness of volition in the manipulator. They assert that the full exercise of the vril power can only be acquired by the constitutional temperament, by hereditarily transmitted organization, and that a female infant of four years old belonging to the Vril-ya races can accomplish feats which a life spent in its practice would not enable the strongest and most skilled mechanician, born out of the pale of the Vril-ya to achieve. . . . I should say, however, that this people have invented certain tubes by which the vril fluid can be conducted towards the object it is meant to destroy, throughout a distance almost indefinite; at least I put it modestly when I say from 500 to 600 miles."

After the First World War a secret society was formed in Germany called the Vril Society with the alchemic Black Sun as their symbol.[10] The concept of the master race fueled the imagination of German fascists in the 1920s and 30s. The 1930 short brochure *Vril: Die kosmische Urkraft* described the Atlanteans as possessors of a spiritual "dynamo-technology," superior to the mechanistic notions of modern science.[IX] This secret society supposedly added to the concepts and notions of Aryan superiority that was expressed most vividly by fascistic German occultists.

See: Lytton, Sir Edward Bulwer. *Vril: The Power of the Coming Race.* New York: Kessinger Publishing, Llc, 2010.

THE BASQUE

The origin of the Basque people who have occupied parts of northern Spain and southern France for centuries is one of the world's oldest mysteries. The Basque language is just as mysterious as the origin of the people who speak it.

Because the Basque language does not relate to any of the Indo-European languages that surround it, it is classified as a language isolate. Historians and language experts believe that Basque is the last surviving pre-Indo-European language

---

[10] The Black Sun, or the *Schwarze Sonne* in German, is an occult symbol depicting a circle containing a sun wheel mosaic. It was an important symbol for fascist occultists for the symbol was even depicted as a floor mosaic in the castle of Wewelsburg, Germany, the spiritual headquarters of the *SS*.

in Western Europe. Basque is spoken by approximately one million people and is the first language to approximately 660,000 people.

For a long period of time the region known as Vasconia enjoyed an amount of self-government up until the French Revolution, and though since 1979 the Basque autonomous community has remained rather autonomous from Spain, the Basque people have maintained the struggle for greater independence. The radical Marxist-Leninist group ETA has led a violent separatist campaign against Spain and France, killing over 800 individuals since 1968. [11]

See: Kurlansky, Mark. *The Basque History of the World: The Story of a Nation*. Boston: Penguin (Non-Classics), 2001.

N17

The Revolutionary Organization 17 November, or N17, was a militant Greek Marxist-Leninist terrorist organization which carried out twenty successful assassinations and over one-hundred attacks from 1973 to 2002 mostly in the city of Athens. N17's attacks were so frequent over the years that it became a regular, almost normal, aspect of Greek politics.

---

[11]The name Basque comes from the Latin *Vasco*. ETA is the acronym for *Euskadi Ta Askatasuna* which translates as the "Basque Homeland and Freedom." ETA declared a ceasefire in 2010.

N17 took its name from the powerful 1973 protest at the Athens Polytechnic against the military *junta* that came to power in 1967. Though the *junta* collapsed in 1974, N17 identified itself as a Marxist revolutionary organization and pursued the policy of political assassination, and 1975 the group successfully assassinated the CIA's station chief Richard Welch.

Throughout the many years underground the group assassinated a US Navy Captain, a US Navy Commander, a US Air Force Sergeant, a British military attaché, and others. The group was tried in the early 2000s, and in 2003 was disbanded with its leaders under arrest and in prison.

See: Kassimeris, George. *Europe's Last Red Terrorists: The Revolutionary Organization 17 November*. London: NYU Press, 2001.

THE TRASH VORTEX

The Great Pacific Garbage Patch also known as the Pacific Trash Vortex is a large system of rotating currents of garbage that deliberately or accidently got into the ocean. The trash vortex is located roughly at 135° to 155°W and 35° to 42°N in the Pacific Ocean.

Most of the trash is made up of plastic and chemical sludge. There are several similar gyres throughout all the oceans with patches of marine debris. Though there were scientists who had predicted that such a debris patch would form, it was not discovered until the late 1990s.

As of this printing nobody really knows how large the patch is, some say it is as large as the state of Texas. As plastics break up into smaller parts they are often swallowed by marine life which may be later consumed by humans.

THE CROSS

The cross is a geometrical figure consisting of one line crossing the other, such as a plus sign, +. It is one of the most ancient pre-historical symbols and is often associated with various Christian denominations, as well as earlier pre-Christian religious and mystical symbolism. The word *cross* is derived from the Latin word *crux* which means "the wooden frame for execution." It was often used for crucifixions of criminals, the most famous crucifixions being Jesus of Nazareth. Later the crux became the symbol for Christianity.[12]

---

[12] Crucifixions are still in use today in certain parts of the world as a method of execution. As of 2011 crucifixions are a form of punishment in the Islamic Republic of Iran under the Iranian criminal law article 195. In 2005 a priest of the Romanian Orthodox Church and four other nuns in Romania were charged with imprisonment leading to death for crucifying a 23-year-old nun, Maricica Irina Cornici. In 2009 Saudi Arabia publicly crucified the corpse of a beheaded man convicted of kidnapping and child molestation.

The Maltese cross is the symbol of the Knights Hospitaller, or the Knights of Malta. The Knights of Malta were a major Christian military order founded in 1099 soon after the First Crusade by the Blessed Gerard, an Amalfi native. Along with the Knights Templar, the Knights Hospitaller where the two strongest and most powerful orders in the Western world engaging in decisive battles with Muslims over control of Jerusalem. The cross's design is structured after the crosses used in the First Crusade of 1095. It is also the official cross of St. John Ambulance as well as the Most Venerable Order of St. John of Jerusalem. It can be found on virtually all rifle units in the United Kingdom.

A Celtic cross is a symbol of a cross with a ring surrounding the intersection; it is found in parts of Ireland and Great Britain. It is often believed that the Celtic Cross was introduced in Ireland by Saint Patrick by combining the pagan symbol for the sun (a ring) with the Christian symbol for Christ (the cross), as a way to ease the newly converted into Christianity. Many of these crosses go back to the 7th century and bear rune inscriptions.

The *swastika* is an equilateral cross with arms bent at right angles in a right-facing or left-facing form. Though it is almost universally recognized as the symbol for fascism, primarily Nazi Germany, its origins date to the Neolithic period. The word "swastika" is a derivative of the Sanskrit word *svastika,* meaning a lucky object. The design can be found in all pre-historic cultures such as the Indo-Aryans, Persians, Slavs, Celts, and Greeks.

In Jainism, the symbol represents the seventh Saint Tirthan-kara Suparsva. All Jain temples and books contain a swas-tika. In pre-Christian Slavic cultures the swastika represented the sun god Svarog, and was called *kolovrat*, signifying the power and majesty of the sun and fire. According to ancient Slavic tradition, when the Kievan Rus' Prince Oleg attacked the city of Constantinople and nailed a shield to the city gates, the shield bore a large red swastika.

Throughout the 20th century the swastika came into wide use in Western Europe – at the height of its popularity it was adopted by the Nazi's in the 1920s. After World War II the symbol represented hate, oppression, and violence to many, and has since been banned in Germany. There have been attempts to ban it in the European Union, however this attempt has been met with great resistance by those who claim that the symbol has been around for over 5,000 years and represents good luck and peace.

The Sun Cross – also known as the wheel cross, Odin's cross and Woden's cross – is an ancient symbol associated with pre-Christian Nordic gods, particularly Odin who was one-eyed with two ravens symbolizing his intelligence. This symbol has also appeared in ancient Egypt, China, the Near East and the Americas before colonization. In Ancient

Greece this symbol stood for sphere or globe and in modern astrology it stands for our planet Earth.

In its pagan usage the sun cross was associated with supreme power and was later appropriated by religions and movements such as Christianity which adopted it as their consecration and inauguration cross. Today this symbol is sometimes used by homeless people in the Western world to indicate: "here you will find food, work, and money," or "here live generous people."

See: Bryce, Derek. *Symbolism of the Celtic Cross.* Felinfach, Lampeter, Dyfed, Wales: Llanerch Enterprises, 1989. *Also see*: Castillo, Dennis. *The Maltese Cross: A Strategic History of Malta (Contributions in Military Studies).* Westport, CT: Praeger Security International Academic Cloth, 2005.

SEPPUKU AND HARA-KIRI

In Japanese samurai culture *seppuku* and *hara-kiri* are a form of ritual suicide by disembowelment. It is often performed in order to rid one of dishonor and if done correctly then it is believed that the dishonor has been lifted.

In Japanese *seppuku* means "stomach cutting," and is performed in an extremely ritualistic manner. Often the one committing the act would wear a white robe, eat his last meal, and then a knife would be placed on his plate, this is the knife with which he will cut his stomach. While the man is performing suicide his second man (the *kaishaku*), often a best friend or enemy, would decapitate him. Before the man commits this ritual it is customary to write a death poem.

The most recent and most popular ritual suicide in Japan took place in 1970 by Yukio Mishima, a Japanese writer and actor who committed hara-kiri in public after a failed coup d'état.

See: Scott-Stokes, Henry. *The life and death of Yukio Mishima*. First Printing ed. New York: Farrar, Straus and Giroux, 1974. *And*: Seward, Jack. *Hara-Kiri: Japanese Ritual Suicide (Tut books)*. Boston: Tuttle Pub, 1968.

THE GEISHA

A Geisha is a traditional female entertainer in Japan whose skills include song and dance. The term derives from the Chinese, meaning one that is talented and skilled.

The traditional role of a geisha is to attend parties or events frequented by men and provide them with humor, light conversation, the recital of poetry or verse, as well as song and dance. Historically girls began their geisha education at the age of seven and were then indebted to their service by a severe contract for many years. Today this practice is no longer used – however the geisha role and profession are still in existence in Japan.

In the West there is confusion regarding the precise role of the geisha, and many often confuse the women with prostitutes. While the geisha may lightly flirt with her male client, there is no sex. This misinformation regarding the geisha and the prostitute may be attributed to the allied forces that used to call prostitutes "geisha girls."

See: Iwasaki, Mineko. *Geisha: A Life*. New York: Washington Square Press, 2003.

AS SLOW AS POSSIBLE

As Slow As Possible (ASLAP), also known as or Organ[2], is a musical piece composed by American composer John Cage. It is the slowest musical work in the world, being played automatically by a six-pipe organ weighed down by sandbags in the abandoned thousand-year old Sankt-Burchardi Church in Halberstadt, Germany. Although the musical piece has only four pages of notes, it is playing so slowly that it will take over six-hundred years until the organ plays its final note. The conceptual work is geared at exploring man's concept of oneself in relation to time, art, and eternity.

THE WALL STREET SWEATER GIRL

In 1968 Francine Gottfried was an employee at Chemical Bank in New York City. Every day she would arrive at the Wall Street subway stop at 1:28 in the afternoon. Being a shapely woman with a figure of 43-23-37 caused crowds of men to wait for her arrival each day. Noticing that she arrived at the same time each day rumors spread of the "Wall Street Sweater Girl" with the shapely figure.

For several weeks in 1968 "girl-watchers" would wait for her arrival to gawk at the young woman. The number of these men grew larger every day until on September 18, 1968 2,000 people awaited her arrival. The next day 5,000 came, and on the third day 10,000 people filled the streets to see the famous girl "sweater girl." According to reports journalists from all over the world with cameras were awaiting the young girl's arrival, people released ticker tape from buildings, and police waited with bullhorns.

For two weeks in September she was the subject of intense media and mania, leading her to quit her job on Wall Street. She later faded into obscurity and became a go-go dancer.

SOVIET BARDS

In 1953 liberal voices within the Russian intelligentsia began to demand for more sincere and honest material in the cultural realm of Soviet production. In December of 1953 the journal *Novy Mir* published Vladimir Pomerantsev's essay "On Sincerity in Literature."[X]

Pomerantsev, a young literary critic, made a bold attack on Socialist-Realism in literature, saying "Sincerity – this is exactly what, in my view, is lacking in some books and plays." Pomerantsev was talking about most books and plays of the time which were still toting the Party line, embracing events and ideas over people.[XI] Pomerantsev's essay however addressed a wider audience, not just the literary community.

Though the "liberal" generation of official Russian authors and poets such as Yevtushenko and Voznesenky were allowed to slightly push the limits and often butted heads with authorities, they were nonetheless kept under strict Union control and highly censored. Despite the fact that the new generation was more prone to craftily criticize the past they looked upon the present and the future through the prescribed prism of Socialist Realism and what is known as *partiinost'*, and many were openly devout Communists.

Their works portrayed Soviet life in a much more humane way with less emphasis on the great deeds of the Soviet people, their ideology nonetheless rested on the foundations of

Marxism-Leninism; their works avoided the starkly poor nature of Soviet existence; they ignored the irony and pretensions contained within their portrayals of familiar scenes and objects of Soviet reality. Thus avoiding social commentary a la Solzhenitsyn, most authors, with the exception of perhaps a few like Andrei Siniavskii churned out rather anodyne fare.[XII]

Artists and musicians not privileged to be members of the top creative unions could not officially exhibit or earn a living from their creative work. The introduction of the tape recorder and the magnetic tape into the easily accessed market challenged the seemingly absolute dominance of the official censors. Social anthropologist Alexie Yurchak describes the phenomenon known as *magnitizdat*:

"Tape recorded music became easily accessible to most young people, even those who did not own a recorder. The songs of bardy (bards) – poets singing to an acoustic guitar – became the first nonofficial cultural objects reproduced in millions of copies and dispersed all over the country by means of home tape-recording."[XIII]

Bard historian Inna Sokolova observed that the genre was formulated by the Soviet intelligentsia in the post-war period.[XIV] It differed from other forms of song in that the author was the composer and performer, with the dominant emphasis being on the poem, thus making the genre fundamentally a literary phenomenon.

Its origins are still largely debatable, yet there is evidence that the bard song was the intellectual offspring of pre-war and pre-revolutionary folklore, Alexander Vertinsky often being cited as the genre's "father."

Despite its murky forerunners, the genre had its post-war creators. These were Alexander Galich, Bulat Okudzhava, and Mikhail Ancharov. All born in the 1920s and participants in the Second World War, they quickly garnered fame and admiration from millions of Soviet citizens who found their poem-songs refreshing, honest and sincere.

These authors had limited musical abilities. Okudzhava for example knew no more than five chords, and the Leningrad bard Alexander Gorodnitsky, who would come to prominence in the early 1960s, never learnt to play the guitar at all. Music was thus an accompaniment, used as a tool for rhythm and atmosphere rather than as an equal element of the song.

The early bards would inspire thousands of youths to start writing songs and playing the guitar. Magnitizdat recordings spread like wildfire across the Soviet Union, and Okudzhava, Galich, and Ancharov became celebrities, composing songs that addressed urban life, history, and honest observations about Soviet realities rooted in the Russian literary tradition. They would influence a second generation of bards that came to prominence in the mid-to-late-1960s, such as Alexander Dolsky, Yuri Vizbor, Yuli Kim, Ada Yakusheva, and Vladimir Vysotsky.

The bards were unofficial artists, perceived as harbingers of truth, giving voice to a society which was yearning for expression and reflection. They were not writing protest-songs, or waging any political resistance. Most of them loved their country and desired to be officially recognized. Yet the social and political circumstance of their creative environment made their work a sort of aesthetic resistance.

Their fame spread not only because of creative lyricism and catchy melodies; rather their works addressed a dark past, casting moral judgments on society and themselves. The social and philosophical songs by Okudzhava, Galich, and others, are their most significant works, and best exemplify the atmosphere of the Thaw and the stagnation which followed afterwards.

The officials were quick to understand the danger of such music. It was impossible to arrest the thousands of people involved in the production, reproduction, and distribution of these tapes, as was the impossibility of arresting the millions of devout listeners. The only method of silencing the bards was through official channels of banning unofficial concerts which were often held in apartments, factories, and open fields in the countryside.

Another affective method of keeping the bards from recognition was to deny access into the Union of Writers or to force them out, as was the case with Galich in 1971, thereby denying the bards the status of being acknowledged artists, labeling the movement amateurish and lacking any social value or competence. The bards were thus not allowed to publish their songs in print, and if they were they appeared highly censored.

The "sincerity" and "honesty" that Pomerantsev and other liberals had hoped would enter official culture dissipated almost immediately after Khrushchev's famous tirade at an exhibition of unorthodox artists at the Manezh Gallery in 1962. Shortly afterwards several Stalinists were restored to prominent cultural posts, while conservatives demanded that all artists be herded into one monolithic union that would be easier for the authorities to police.[XV] What resulted was a struggle between the liberals and the conservatives, a struggle that continued throughout most of the later Soviet period.

Despite the authorities' attempts at controlling the bard movement, by the 1960s it was impossible to stop the dissemination of the magnitizdat. In 1960 only 128,000 tape-recorders were made available to the Soviet public, by 1965 nearly 500,000 were available, and by 1970 their number topped 1 million.[XVI] The compact recorders, whose cost was roughly equivalent to an engineer's monthly salary, moved, incognito, from one kitchen concert to the next, nestled inside backpacks on the their owners' backs.[XVII]

In the mid-1950s, influenced by the poem-songs of Okudzhava, Russian bard Alexander Dolsky acquired his first guitar by trading a collection of semiprecious stones, or as Dolsky would later put it: "I gave away a green rock in exchange for communication with the gods."

See: Feldbrugge, F. J. M. Feldbrugge, and Ferdinand J. M. Feldbrugge. *Samizdat & Political Dissent in the Soviet Union*. Boston: Kluwer Law International, 1975.

THE MARTINI

The martini is a popular drink that is mostly consumed in the United States and England and other English-speaking countries. Its origins are somewhat mysterious; some claim that the martini was discovered by a lucky miner during the California Gold Rush of 1849. According to the legend the miner was traveling through the city of Martinez, freshly rich from a good find, when a local barman showed him a local concoction, known as the Martinez Special.

However, it is more likely that the martini was invented sometime in the mid-1860s when Martini & Rossi created the *Martini Rosso* dry vermouth, and was most likely created in the US or the UK by mixing gin with that particular brand of Martini vermouth.

The martini is prepared in several different methods, perhaps the most common is the Dry Martini, which is a well shaken or stirred mix of ice, gin, and dry vermouth served with a twist or an olive. To make the martini a Dirty Dry Martini typically two tablespoons of olive brine are added.

THE CALENDAR

Calendars as systems of organizing days have existed throughout the history of mankind. In 2007 researchers examining an ancient temple in Peru discovered a 4,200-year-old calendar. The oldest calendar that is still in-use is the Hindu calendar which though undergoing various changes throughout the centuries has been used since 3100 BC.

The Julian calendar was a system of measuring days and years in ancient Rome. It was introduced as a reform by Julius Caesar in 46 BC and remained active into the beginning of the 20th century in some countries.

Russia did not switch to the Gregorian calendar until 1918. To this day when reading historical documents about Imperial Russia or nations that used the Julian into the 20th century one must note "OS" for "Old Style" when referring to the Julian and "NS" for "New Style." The Russian Revolution took place on October 25, 1917 OS but on November 7, 1918 NS.

See: Duncan, David Ewing. *Calendar: Humanity's Epic Struggle to Determine a True and Accurate Ye*. Newark: See Notes, 1998.

ADWAITA

Adwaita was possibly the oldest living animal in the world. Born sometime around 1750, the Aldabra giant tortoise was the pet of General Robert Clive of the British East India Company. After spending some time on Clive's estate it was moved to the zoo in 1875, where it lived until its death from liver failure in 2006. After carbon dating its shell scientists revealed that it was around 225 years old.

There are several species of living organisms that can live for a very long time in comparison to human beings and some have even outlived the normal lifespan of their own species.

The Great Basin Bristlecone Pine, named Methuselah, can live over 4,800 years, while olive trees can live up to 2,000 years. Some mollusks live up to 400 years, koi fish can live to 220, Red Sea Urchins can live over 100, and tortoises can live over 180.

Perhaps the most fascinating organism is the *Turritopsis nutricula* (a hydrozoan) which is biologically immortal.

COUNT OF SAINT GERMAIN

The Count of Saint Germain is a mysterious figure that appeared upon the European courtly scene in the eighteenth century. He was known as an eccentric mystic whom many believed to be immortal and later an Ascended Master in the school of Theosophy.

The famed Venetian adventurer Giacomo Casanova wrote of the Count's supposed alchemical prowess in his memoirs:

"This extraordinary man, intended by nature to be the king of imposters and quacks, would say in an easy, assured manner that he was three hundred years old, that he knew the secret of the Universal Medicine, that he possessed a mastery over nature, that he could melt diamonds, professing himself capable of forming, out of ten or twelve small diamonds, one large one of the finest water without any loss of weight."

Throughout history many have claimed to have encountered Saint Germain, including Annie Besant, C.W. Leadbeater, Guy Ballard, and Dorothy Lean. During one of his trances, the American prophet Edgar Cayce was asked if Saint Germian was present to which Cayce responded: "when needed."

THE SIN-EATER

A sin-eater is a person who through rituals involving food and drink "eats" the sins of a dying or deceased person, in this manner taking upon oneself the burden of their sins. According to Bertram Puckle, the sin-eater would place some sort of food, typically crumbs or dried pieces of bread, upon the person's chest, perform a ritual, then eat the food.

In the 1926 study *Funeral Customs* Puckle writes:

"Abhorred by the superstitious villagers as a thing unclean, the sin-eater cut himself off from all social intercourse with his fellow creatures by reason of the life he had chosen; he lived as a rule in a remote place by himself, and those who chanced to meet him avoided him as they would a leper. This unfortunate was held to be the associate of evil spirits, and given to witchcraft, incantations and unholy practices; only when a death took place did they seek him out, and when his purpose was accomplished they burned the wooden bowl and platter from which he had eaten the food handed across, or placed on the corpse for his consumption."[XVIII]

Sin-eating has been virtually wiped out of existence, and if it does exist then only in secrecy. The rituals of sin-eating were practiced in parts of England, Scotland, and into the twentieth-century in parts of Wales and the Welsh Marches. The practice was forbidden by the church, but often the vicar of the towns turned a blind eye to the unusual habit. It is believed that a well-off English farmer Richard Munslow was England's last sin-eater who died in 1906 and was buried in Ratlinghope Church.

LIPOGRAMMATIC NOVELS

In 1939 the author Ernest Vincent Wright published *Gadbsy*, a novel of over 50,000 words without using the letter *e*. A novel that avoids a letter or certain letters is called a lipogrammatic novel. A part from *Gadsby:*

"But a human brain is not in that class. Constantly throbbing and pulsating, it rapidly forms opinions; attaining an ability of its own; a fact which is startlingly shown by an occasional child "prodigy" in music or school work. And as, with our dumb animals, a child's inability convincingly to impart its thoughts to us, should not class it as ignorant."

HIROO ONODA

Hiroo Onoda is a former Japanese spy who fought in World War II, but unlike everyone else in the Japanese military, Onoda did not surrender until 1974. In 1944 while on a military intelligence mission on Lubang Island in the Philippines he was ordered to do everything in his power to hamper enemy attacks on the island and under no circumstances was he to surrender or commit suicide.

Beginning in 1945 Onoda and three other soldiers, Akatsu, Shimada, and Kozuka, lived in the mountains ignoring the leaflets that were being dropped informing soldiers that the war was over. Private Akatsu left the three soldiers and surrendered to Filipino forces in 1950. Throughout the 1950s Onoda and the two other soldiers continued guerilla activities throughout the Philippines such as setting the rice fields on fire and conducting shoot-outs with locals and police. They ignored letters and photographs of family members that were dropped on them, thinking it to be a hoax.

Shimada was killed in 1954 after a shoot-out with a search party. In 1959 Onoda and Kozuka were officially declared dead, but after a search party could not find any dead bodies some people suspected that the two were still alive. Kozuka appeared in 1972 but was killed in a shootout with the Filipino police.

Onoda become something of a legend in his native Japan. Numerous search parties could not find him, until in 1974 a young Japanese university dropout named Suzuki went on a tour of the Philippines, telling his friends that he was going to search for Lieutenant Onoda, a panda, and the Abdominal Snowman in that order. Soon Suzuki found the soldier and informed the Japanese media of Onoda's existence.

It was not until Onoda's commanding officer, Major Taniguchi, came out of retirement that and flew to Lubang to personally inform the soldier that the war was indeed over that he surrendered. Onoda has since released an autobiography, *No Surrender: My Thirty-Year War*. Onoda ran a camp for young children, teaching them about nature and survival techniques. He died in 2014.

See: Onoda, Hiroo. *No Surrender: My Thirty-Year War (Bluejacket Books)*. Annapolis, Md.: Us Naval Institute Press, 1999.

GREEN CHILDREN OF WOOLPIT

In the twelfth-century two strange children were discovered cowering in a hole near a cave in Woolpit, England. The villagers were all astonished at the strange appearance of the two, for their skin had a bizarre green hue. When the villagers tried to speak with them the children appeared frightened and spoke in an unintelligible language.

When the villagers attempted to feed the children, they would only eat green beans and it took several months for the children to acquire a taste for bread. The boy died fairly quickly, but after some time the young girl adjusted to her life, began to lose the green color, and learned English.

When she became a healthy woman and married she revealed what she had remembered of her life prior to coming to Woolpit. She claimed the young boy was her brother, and that they lived in an underground cavernous world called Saint Martins Land, where everyone was colored green and the sun never rose and that the two wondered off to the sound of bells until they were on land and could not find their way back.

TSAR BOMBA

The Tsar Bomba, or the Tsar Bomb, is the largest hydrogen bomb and nuclear weapon ever detonated. It was developed by the Soviet Union with a blast yield of 50 megatons of TNT, and tested on October 30, 1961 in the Novaya Zemlya archipelago. The archipelago was the site of massive nuclear testing by the Soviets, over 200 detonations with over 260 megatons of TNT occurred there. The Tsar Bomb was named "Tsar" because of its grandiose design.

Novaya Zemlya, which in Russian means "new land," became a designated nuclear test site in September 1954 and throughout the 50s and 60s the area had over 220 nuclear detonations. According to Sara Pratt of the Lamont-Doherty Earth Observatory at Columbia University's Earth Institute, the Soviet Union conducted 130 underwater, atmospheric and underground nuclear tests at Novaya Zemlya over a period of 35 years, some of which involved multiple explosions.

In all, 224 nuclear devices were detonated, amounting to 265 megatons of explosive energy. By comparison, all of the explosives detonated over the course of World War II, including the August 1945 detonations of two U.S. nuclear bombs over Japan, amounted to two megatons.[XIX] These experiments and tests did not become public knowledge until the *glasnost* reforms of the late 1980s.

See: Rhodes, Richard. *Arsenals of Folly: The Making of the Nuclear Arms Race (Vintage)*. 2008. Reprint. New York: Vintage, 2008.

CADAVER SYNOD

In January 897 Pope Stephen VI (VII) ordered that the body of his predecessor Pope Formosus be exhumed and put on trial. The trial was politically motivated, largely due to the hatred of Formosus by the Spoletens.

Propped upon a throne, the corpse of Formosus was charged with several offences while a living deacon was put in charge of answering for the corpse. He was found guilty of being illegally crowned Pope, all of his acts were squashed, and the three fingers he used for consecration were removed. Formosus' papal vestments were torn from his body and the corpse was cast to a cemetery designated for strangers and foreigners.

Several days later the body was thrown into the Tiber River. The body was rescued by a monk and reinterred in St. Peter's. Pope Stephen VI (VII) was deposed and murdered in prison. Stephen's successor, Pope Theodore II, annulled the previous decisions of the Cadaver Synod.

THE PENTAGRAM

The pentagram is an ancient star-polygon with 5 edges and vertices and a 36 degree internal angle. In Greek the word *penta* means five and *gramma* means "what is written." The first recorded pentagram appears in ancient Mesopotamian writings dating back to 3000BC. It has been the dominating symbol for many groups, organizations, religions, sects, and cults, and is most notably associated with the Pythagoreans, Cabalists, Masons, Gnostics, Satanists, and Wiccans.

The mysticism and occultism associated with the pentagram has much to do with the number 5, a prime number and the sum of 2 and 3, as well as 1 and 4. For early Greek philosophers and mystics these five vertices represented the five classical elements of the universe.[13]

---

[13] The classical elements were developed in antiquity and supposedly are what make the essential principles of which everything consists of and from which everything is based. Each culture, historic period, and intellectual and scientific school has developed their own elements from which everything on this planet consists and almost all of them are the same. For example the classical elements of Ancient Greece were Air (Aer, ἀήρ), Water (Hydor, ὕδωρ), Heat (Heile, ἑιλή), Earth (Gaia, Γαια), and the Divine (Hieron, ἱερόν); the Tibetan elements are very similar, being Air, Water, Fire, Earth, and Space. In some cultures Air is referred to as Wind and Space is often described as Void and Essence.

For the Greek followers of Pythagoras harmony and balance were the principles that determined the order of the cosmos. The Pythagoreans divided numbers into odd and even, symbolizing the balance of the universe, which they saw as associated with the balance of masculinity (odd) and femininity (even).[14] Thus for the Pythagoreans the pentagram represented a geometrical and cosmological perfection and was written with the two vertices pointed upwards, symbolizing the Pythagorean doctrine of *Pentemychos* authored by the sixth-century ancient Greek thinker Pherecydes of Syros, a text which has been lost.[15] In the *Pentemychos* the five vertices represented the five chambers of the universe, according to scholars of philosophy these vertices' were the place where the first pre-cosmic offspring had to be placed in order for the cosmos to appear.

---

[14] The third-century Christian theologian and Bishop of Rome Hippolytus famously wrote of this numerological philosophy: "Number is the first principle, a thing which is undefined, incomprehensible, having in itself all numbers which could reach infinity in amount. And the first principle of numbers is in substance the first monad, which is a male monad, begetting as a father all other numbers." Aristotle explained the same concept in much simpler verse in *Metaphysics*: "...the first principles are ten, named according to the following table: finite and infinite, even and odd, one and many, right and left, male and female, rest and motion, straight and crooked, light and darkness, good and bad, square and oblong."

[15] The *Pentemychos* is also called the *Heptamychos*. Aristotle described the work as a mixture of mysticism and Greek philosophy.

For the Romans the pentagram could have represented Salvs, the goddess of health, if the letters S A L V S were inscribed into the five points. Salvs was often depicted on the gold and silver of Nero's period, and it is recorded that the supposedly mad emperor made vows before the goddess.

For the early Christians the pentagram's five points were associated with the five wounds of Christ, and some early Christians would wear the pentagram as an amulet instead of the cross. This association lasted until the twelfth-century when the Church authorities instituted the cross as the official symbol for the religion, associating Christ's crucifixion with the symbolism of the Christian faith (see *The Cross*). Nevertheless, the pentagram can be found within certain Christian churches, temples, odes, ballads, and manuscripts up to the thirteenth-century throughout Western and Eastern Europe, and the twelfth-century Christian mystical sect known as the Cathars apparently used the pentagram in their secret rituals.[16]

---

[16] The Cathars were divided into two groups, the perfecti, or Parfaits, and the *credentes*, the "believers." The *perfecti* symbolized the core, dedicated, "pure," ascetics who lived in simplicity and expounded a vegan lifestyle. Their numbers were much smaller than the credentes, who in comparison lived relatively normal lives. The ritual that involved the pentagram was called the Consolamentum, which was a baptism of the soul, in which the future perfecti was absolved, liberated from this world, dawned simple black robes and led an exemplar life of purity. It is said that the Church Caves of Ornolac were the supposed headquarters of the Cathar religion. Interestingly, one of

According to the French historian Antonin Gadal, when the Cathars exercised the final initiation of the believer they took the novice to the Bethlehem cave in Ornolac where the Cathar was made a *perfecti*, or a perfect one, by stepping inside a large pentagram carved into the cave of the wall. The harmonious nature of the pentagram can be seen in Leonardo da Vinci's drawing often called the *Vitruvian Man* created in the late 1480s.[17]

The drawing is supposed to represent the ideal proportions of man according to the classical order of architecture, with arms and legs outstretched. If a pentagram is placed directly over the image it will be seen that the outstretched arms and legs represent the four vertices, while the head represents the fifth pointing upwards.

Among European occultists the pentagram has had dark connotations. If the pentagram was upside down or bent to certain degrees it could attract evil forces. It can also be interpreted as the fall of man from heights to depths of darkness, a deviation from the natural order. Franz Hartmann wrote in his 1895 work *Magic, White and Black*:

---

the rituals involved the placing of the hands on a dying persons head or on another perfecti, through which the spirit moved, a practice which was said to have been passed down directly from Jesus Christ.
[17] The drawing has been called the *Vitruvian Man* for it is accompanied by da Vinci's notes on the Roman architect and writer Marcus Vitruvius Pollio (80-15BC).

". . .let us keep the star always pointed upright . . . to heaven, for it is the seat of wisdom, and if the figure is reversed, perversion and evil will be the result."[18]

Satanists indeed reverse the pentagram, with the two bottom points facing up symbolic for the horns of Lucifer and the bottom point facing down symbolizing Lucifer's beard. According to the British occultist Aleister Crowley a reversed pentagram symbolizes the descent of spirit into matter.[19]

JUST ADD WATER

Instant noodles or "Instant ramen" have been available in Asia for centuries; however it was not until 1958 when the Japanese inventor Momofuko Ando made the first modern instant noodles with which we are familiar with today. Ando released his creation under the name Chikin Ramen.

---

[18] Hartmann (1838-1912) was a German occultist, the founder of the German Theosophical Society, and the translator of the *Bhagavad Gita* into the German. He was the co-founder of the international fraternal organization known the Ordo Templi Orientis, of which Crowley (*see next footnote*) was a member.

[19] Edward Alexander Crowley (1875-1947), more commonly known as Aliester Crowley, often claimed to be the wickedest man in the world was an English occultist who founded the religious philosophy of Thelema. An influential member of the Hermetic Order of the Golden Dawn, Crowley was a controversial figure who was known for his wild sexual exploits and experimentations with drugs.

In 1971 Nissin released their famous Cup Noodles, which are instant noodles in a cup which when filled with boiling water instantly cooked the noodles. According to a 2005 statistic approximately 85 billion servings of instant noodles are eaten every year and it is considered one of the most important Japanese inventions of the century. China consumed over 40 billion packages of instant noodles every year, followed by Indonesia by 14 billion and Japan by 5 billion.

The success of instant noodles is largely due to their low costs, which allows them to be purchased by all segments of the population. Low costs are also associated with the growing popularity of instant noodles throughout the world, making it the most popular instant food.

Instant coffee has also seen a large growth in the last twenty years. Though many associated instant coffee with the 1930s, it is said that the earliest version was concocted in Britain around the 1770s, when the British government granted a patent for a "coffee compound." The instant coffee was made by extracting all the water from the coffee, then later scraping the residue off the stainless steel drums. The taste was bitter and did not resemble a freshly brewed cup of coffee.

In 1901 Satori Kato, a Japanese chemist who was working in the United States at the time came up with a powdered substance that became known as instant coffee and began to market it in 1910. Several companies including Nescafe, came out with their own versions of instant coffee, but no significant advances were made until the 1960s, when the process of freeze-drying was introduced and revolutionized the industry.

The most efficient, calorie-packed, instant foods are the military MRE's, short for "Meal-Ready-To-Eat."[20]   They are small self-contained individual field rations in lightweight packaging primarily used by the United States military. Produced in all kinds of entrees, including beef ravioli, pork rib, chicken breast, etc., soldiers only need to pour water into the packets and the contents cook on their own.

THE DESPOSYNI

The Desposyni are the relatives of Jesus Christ.   It is believed that Christ's relatives became followers of his teachings and later the leaders of the early Christian church into the third-century.   In the New Testament there are several mentions of his "brethren."

Some of these brethren are mentioned by name – primarily James, Joseph, Simon, and Jude. But the nature of the term brethren has been the subject of theological debate since the earliest times of the Bible. In the Semitic languages brethren

---

[20] Prior to 1981 the military used "Meal, Combat, Individual Rations" (MCI), which were canned, and would often be damaged or spoiled.

may be used loosely, suggesting not just the blood relatives, but also step-relatives, distant and near relatives, and perhaps even acquaintances.

It is believed that Jesus had one or more sisters. Perhaps the most important alleged member of Jesus's immediate family was "the brother of the Lord" James – known often as Saint James the Just. He was the first Bishop of Jerusalem and the author of the Epistle of James in the New Testament. With the publication of the *Da Vinci Code* in 2003 there was a renewed interest and debate into the bloodline of Jesus Christ.

See: Hanson, Ph.D., and Kenneth. *Blood Kin of Jesus: James and the Lost Jewish Church*. Beltsville, MD: Council Oak Books, 2009.

THE KILLING OF THE FLESH

Mortification is the act of putting the human flesh through physical pain in order to conduct penance for sins, to atone, and reach a communion with God through suffering. The word mortification stems from the Latin *mortis*, meaning dying, and *mortificare*, meaning to cause death. Literally the term translates as the killing of the flesh.

Forms of mortification can be found in the ascetic practices of Eastern religions such as Hinduism, Buddhism, Shia and Sufi Islam. In the West mortification seems more prevalent and was a predominant form of ascetic practice in the early years of the Christian church. The wearing of a *cilice* and sacks of leather over the body to experience dreadful heat and bodily irritation was common for monks, ascetics, church leaders, and even lay persons and nobility.

The eleventh-century Italian Saint Petrus Damiani wrote much on the subject of Christian theology, including on the role of mortification in relation to the spirit. In his treatise *The Monastic Ideal*, Damiani explained the logic behind harsh forms of self-inflicted pain:

"And so there is nothing but the love of God and the mortification of yourselves. . . The man who is wise and earnestly intent on guarding his salvation watches always with such great solicitude to repress his vices that with the belt of perfect mortification he girds his loins and his reins, his belly as well as his flanks, on all sides." [21]

Among the lesser known ascetics was a zealously faithful fifth-century Syrian who went by the name of Baradatus. Almost nothing is known about him, and what little information we do possess comes from the writings of Theodoret the Bishop of Cyrhhus, who wrote of Baradatus' fascinating forms of mortification in his *Religious History*.

---

[21] Born in Ravenna, Petrus Damiani (1007-1072) is considered one of the most admired of Italian saints, so much so that when the great Dante Alighieri wrote the *Divina Commedia* in the fourteenth-century he placed Damiani in the Seventh Sphere of *Paradiso*, the sphere of Saturn where the contemplatives reside.

Baradatus built a small lattice coffin-like structure made of interwoven pieces of wood. Apparently the device was fashioned in such a way that it had many openings so as to be open to all the conditions of the weather. Theodoret writes that the box:

". . . no way conformed to the dimensions of a human body, but in which he had to live bent double, for neither its depth nor its length was of a convenient size."

The monk later devised a much more unbearable contraction, a suite made out of leather which covered his entire body, including the face, which he wore while standing in the desert with hands outstretched, the heat causing terrible blisters to his flesh.

Acts of self-inflicted pain and torture can be attributed to the social circumstances of the times and the religious mindset. For people of the early church as well as the medieval period, the concepts of good and evil were very much real, and the second coming of Christ was believed to occur at any moment.

With disease and famine rampant people often felt they had sinned against God and only voluntary mortification relieved such sins. The eleventh-century German mystic Heinrich Suso wrote of his own flagellation through the third-person:

"He [Suso] shut himself in his cell and stripped himself naked, and took his scourge with the sharp spikes, and beat himself on the body and on the arms and on the legs, till blood poured off him as from a man who had been cupped. One of the spikes on the scourge was bent like a hook, and whatever flesh it caught tore off. He beat himself so hard that the scourge broke into three pieces and the points flew against the wall. He stood there bleeding and gazed at himself. It was such a wretched sight that he was reminded in many ways of the appearance of the beloved Christ, when he was fearfully beaten. Out of pity for himself, he began to weep bitterly. And he knelt down, naked and covered in blood, in the frosty air, and prayed to God to wipe out his sins from before his gentle eyes."XX [22]

Writing in his ground-breaking history of the Roman Empire, the great British historian Edward Gibbon described the

---

[22] Heinrich Suso, also known as the Blessed Henry Suso, Amandus, and Heinrich Seuese, was born in Uberlingen in 1300. He was a mystic and a writer who from the age of thirteen became a Dominican, and by the time he was eighteen had dedicated his life to studying mystical philosophy, as a servant of what he called the "Eternal Wisdom." He left the world several writings amongst which *A Little Book of Eternal Wisdom* exercised a large influence over men of the medieval age. Suso was known for his extreme forms of mortification. At one point in his life he pierced the flesh above his heart and imprinted "Jesus Christ" upon it, a scar that forever remained on his chest. Suso often wore hairshirts (a shirt made of extremely course and irritable material) and designed elaborate torture devices for himself such as a slack-like device with iron nails piercing into the skin. In the winters Suso slept on the cold earth and froze into the nights. It has also been suggested that he never bathed.

bizarre mathematics used to estimate what would alleviate sins:

"By a fantastic arithmetic, a year of penance was taxed at three thousand lashes; and such was the skill and patience of a famous hermit, St. Dominic of the iron Cuirass [Dominicus Loricatus], that in six days he could discharge an entire century, by a whipping of three hundred thousand stripes. His example was followed by many penitents of both sexes; and, as a vicarious sacrifice was accepted, a sturdy disciplinarian might expiate on his own back the sins of his benefactors. These compensations of the purse and the person introduced, in the eleventh century, a more honorable mode of satisfaction."[XXI]

Dominicus Loricatus performed these lashes while reciting the entire Pslater, with 100 lashes per each psalm, which he performed over a six day period during Lent, redeeming 100 years of sin, thus 300,000 self-inflicted strokes. It has been estimated that at this rate he inflicted 41 lashes per minute, 2,500 lashes per hour, and 50,000 lashes per day assuming he was awake for 20 hours a day. The fourteenth-century Italian mystic Saint Catherine of Sienna, who also practiced extreme fasting called inedia (see *Inedia*), would scourge herself in the manner of Loricatus thrice daily. [23]

---

[23] Dominicus Loricatus (955-1060) may have been driven by a tremendous guilt. When he was young his uncle bribed a local bishop in order for the young Dominic to get into the Benedictine order. For

There were times when mortification took the form of a public penance. In November of 1260 an epidemic of mass-flagellation began in Perugia, Italy. Thousands of men of all social ranks from nights to peasants walked naked through the city scourging their person, led by the Bishop and the priests. Up to 10,000 people marched through Modena, Bologna, Reggio, and Parma, inflicting pain upon their person in procession. This epidemic spread to Germany, and created many flagellant cults. The cult of flagellation was banned by the Pope in 1261, but the movement gained momentum once more during the bubonic plague in the mid fourteenth-century.

Though there are no longer mass movements of flagellation as during the years of the plagues there are still people who individually practice this form of penance, and there are many online communities in which flagellants share vivid descriptions of their mortification.

In the town of Guardia Sanframondi in Italy, a penitential rite takes place every seven years. It begins with a series of religious scenes followed by a choir procession which is then followed by the *flagellanti* who beat themselves with metallic sticks and the *battenti* (beaters) who beat themselves with a

---

this reason he vowed to perform penance for the rest of his life. He often wore a coat of mail, or a *lorica*, and thus owes his name Loricatus to this self-inflicted torture.

sponge fitted with metallic spikes. The flagellants are anonymous for they wear hoods and robes; these robes become heavily stained with blood as they walk through the village streets scourging themselves.

In the United States the Los Penitentes are a secret society which some claim dates back to the Spanish colonization of North America. The society today is made up of Roman Catholic men in the Northern New Mexico and southern Colorado area. These men get together in small temples called *morada's* to atone for their sins by flagellating each other with whips called the *disciplina*. They also carry heavy crosses; bind their bodies to large crosses, tying limbs to hinder the circulation of the blood. Up until the 1890s this society was open and these actions were done in public, but in 1890 the church tried to disband the fraternal society and it thus went into secrecy.

The Catholic religious order Opus Dei encourages its members to engage in voluntary acts of mortification, especially the use of the *cilice*, a small metal chain with prongs that is often worn around the thigh and the *discipline*, a cord-like whip made from wool that is used on the bare body.

See: Favazza, Armando R.. *Bodies under Siege: Self-mutilation and Body Modification in Culture and Psychiatry*. second edition ed. Baltimore: The Johns Hopkins University Press, 1996.

BAPHOMET

Baphomet, also known as the Sabbatic Goat, is the name of a pagan god often associated with the occult. Though the name had been around since the early 1000s AD, it was first recorded in the transcripts of the Inquisition of the Knights Templar in the early 1300s as a pagan idol which the Templar's had allegedly worshiped. In *Narratives of Sorcery and Magic* the nineteenth-century writer Thomas Wright wrote:

"Another charge in the accusation of the Templars seems to have been to a great degree proved by the depositions of witnesses[:] the idol or head which they are said to have worshipped, but the real character or meaning of which we are totally unable to explain. Many Templars confessed to having seen this idol, but as they described it differently, we must suppose that it was not in all cases represented under the same form. Some said it was a frightful head, with long beard and sparkling eyes; others said it was a man's skull; some described it as having three faces; some said it was of wood, and others of metal; one witness described it as a painting (tabula picta) representing the image of a man (imago hominis) and said that when it was shown to him, he was ordered to 'adore Christ, his creator.' According to some it was a gilt figure, either of wood or metal; while others described it as painted black and white. According to another deposition, the idol had four feet, two before and two behind; the one belonging to the order at Paris, was said to be a silver head, with two faces and a beard. The novices of the order were told always to regard this idol as their saviour. Deodatus Jaffet, a knight from the south of France, who had been received at Pedenat, deposed that the person who in his case performed the ceremonies of reception, showed him a head or idol, which appeared to have three faces, and said, 'You must adore this as your saviour, and the saviour of the order of the Temple' and that he was made to worship the idol, saying, 'Blessed be he who shall save my soul.' Cettus Ragonis, a knight received at Rome in a chamber of the palace of the Lateran, gave a somewhat similar account. Many other witnesses spoke of having seen these heads, which, however, were, perhaps, not shown to everybody, for the greatest number of those who spoke on this subject, said that they had heard speak of the head, but that they had never seen it themselves; and many of them declared their disbelief in its existence. A friar minor deposed in England that an English Templar had assured him that in that country the order had four principal idols, one at London, in the Sacristy of the Temple, another at Bristelham, a third at Brueria (Bruern in Lincolnshire), and a fourth beyond the Humber."[XXII]

Scholars and occultists have suggested that the Baphomet which the Templars supposedly worshipped was derived from Pan, an ancient god of nature, who is often depicted as half-man half-goat, with horns, and hoofs. The eighteenth-century

Austrian Orientalist Baron Joseph von Hammer-Pürgstall discovered an inscription in Burgandy on a coffer, which he claimed proved that the name of Baphomet derived from two Ancient Greek terms, meaning "Baptism of Metis."[24]

The French occultist Eliphas Levi is perhaps best known for his depiction of Baphomet as the *Sabbatic Goat in his Dogme et Rituel de la Haute Magie*, published in 1855. The origin of the word is heatedly debated. Fringe conspiracy theorists believe that most secret societies worship Baphomet.

See: Stephen, and A Dafoe. *Unholy Worship? The Myth of the Baphomet, Templar, Freemason connection*. China: Templar Books, 1998.

THE SONNET

A sonnet is a poetic form that originates in European lyric poetry. The term is derived from the Occitan word *sonet* and the Italian word *sonetto*, each meaning "little song." The only original Occitan sonnet to survive is by Lanfranchi da Pistoia from 1280, employing the a-b-a-b-, a-b-a-b-, c-d-cd-cd rhyme scheme.[25] The typical sonnet is of fourteen lines with a strict

---

[24] *Metis* in Ancient Greek means "wisdom, skill, craft." Metis is also the name of Zeus's first wife.

[25] A famous Occitan sonnet dates to the 1300s and is written by Jean de Nostredame in honor of Robert of Naples. Jean de Nostredame (1522-c.1576) was the younger brother of world-renowned physician and seer Michel de Nostredame, commonly referred to as Nostradamus.

rhyme scheme, for example the Shakespearean sonnet has the following rhyme scheme: a-b-a-b, c-d-c-d, e-f-e-f, g-g-. The Italian version of the sonnet was created by Giacomo da Lentini in the thirteenth-century, a senior poet at the Sicilian School at the court of the Holy Roman emperor Frederick II. Sir Thomas Wyatt introduced the sonnet to the English speaking world in the sixteenth century with Italian-to-English translations of Petrarch, but it was Henry Howard the Earl of Surrey who gave it the English rhyme scheme.

INEDIA

In Latin inedia means "to fast" but in modern terminology has often been attributed to the mystical and religious practice of abstaining from food and water with the idea that humans do not need nutrition in order to sustain life. This concept was originally applied to Christian saints and mystics who practiced severe austerities in relation to food and lived only off the Eucharist.[26]

Christians living off the Eucharist alone go as far back as the fifth-century; however it was not until the twelfth and thirteenth-centuries that the mystics of the Eucharist become a source of veneration, as was the case the thirteenth-century mystic Alpai of Cudot denied herself any food except for the

---

[26] See the entries on *The Pillar Saints* and *Mortification*.

Echarist, as well as the fifteenth-century patron saint of Swit-
zerland Nicholas of Flüe. The fourteenth-century theologian
and lay Dominican Catherine of Siena chose to eat nothing
but the Eucharist in her last years.

Most Christian female mystics who practiced inedia seem
to share similar life situations. Most became ill or suffer a
tragic injury as children which leaves them disabled and bedridden for the rest of their lives, during which the last fifteen
or so years are spent living only off the Eucharist; while living
off the Eucharist many experienced visions and stigmata, but
many also are exceptionally under nourished, lose a large
amount of weight, and verge upon death.

Such was the case with the fourteenth-century Dutch Saint
Lidwina, who broke her rib during an ice skating accident as
a child. After becoming bedridden she lived only off apples,
later only off river water, and later supposedly only from the
Eucharist.

One of the most famous modern mystics of the Eucharist
was Alexandrina Maria da Costa. Born in 1904 in Balasar,
Portugal, the young girl suffered a terrifying fall from her win-
dow at the age fourteen when three men tried to break into
her room to rape her. The fall broke her spine and Alexandrina suffered gradual paralysis until she was permanently
confined to her bed in 1925.

For about thirteen years starting in 1942 up to her painful
death it is said that Alexandrina received no food except for

the Eucharist, though according to her official Vatican biography at one point she weighed in at only seventy-three pounds.

A similar tale is of Maria Domenica Lazzeri, born in 1815 in Capriana, Italy. Like Alexandrina she became bedridden in 1833 and ate nothing except for the Eucharist for the remaining thirteen years of her life.

Even more extreme is the New Age concept of Breatharianism, which claims that nutrition does not need to come from food or water but rather from the sun or some sort of life force called *prana*.[27]

Beginning in the 1980s several New Age mystics have claimed to have lived completely off the energy of the sun and have not consumed any food. Biologically this is impossible since the organs begin to fail leading to certain death within weeks, as was the case with several hardcore followers in the 1990s.

MOBILE PHONE

The precursor to today's mobile phone was the radiophone of the 1930s often used by civilian police and the military during wars and conflicts. In 1946 Motorola in conjuncture with

---

[27] *Prana* (प्राण) is a Sanskrit word for "vital force" and is a central concept in Yoga.

Bell System operated the first mobile telephone system (MTS) in the United States, and in 1962 Bell System created the first automatic system offering automatic dialing to and from a mobile telephone.

The first public commercial mobile phone network was launched in 1971 in Finland called the Autoradiopuhelin (ARP). By 1978 ARP was available in every single part of Finland with over 130 base stations. In 1981 ARP was being gradually replaced by the NMT, the Nordic Mobile Telephony, which was the first fully automatic cellular phone system. By 2000 ARP was fully phased out because of congestion and the more modern NMT has become the dominant system throughout Finland.

On October 13, 1983 the first commercial wireless call in the United States was made on the Motorola DynaTAC 8000X by Bob Barnett to the grandson of Alexander Graham Bell. The phone is considered a revolutionary step in mobile communications. In 1984 its retail price was $3,995. A Nielsen research study has hypothesized that by 2011 one in two American's will have a smartphone.

See: Agar, Jon. *Constant touch: A global history of the mobile phone.*. Cambridge: Icon Books, 2003.

ANGLER FISH

Often considered the ugliest creature in the waters, the anglerfish live in open water, deep seas, and on the continental shelf. They are in the order of Lophiiformes, in the class of Actinopterygii. The deep-sea angler's live a strange and bizarre life whose mating rituals have been described as forms of sexual suicide. Living in the pitch-black darkness of the deep seas, male angler fish are called dwarf males because they are much smaller than their female counterparts.

The females have a fleshy growth from their heads that acts as a lure, emitting something like a perfume which is picked up by the large nostrils of the dwarf males. The males attach themselves to the back or side of the female, their epidermal tissues and circulatory systems fuse. After this the male dwarfs become an organ of the female. Their blood supply and breathing link together, the male's eyes and digestive systems fail, and they degenerate into a pair of sperm-producing testicles. Whenever an angler fish is depicted it is most typically the female version which is larger.

See: Koslow, J. Anthony. *The silent deep: the discovery, ecology and conservation of the deep sea*. Chicago: University Of Chicago Press, 2007.

VENDEÉ GLOBE

The Vendeé Globe is a round-the-world single handed yacht race without any stopovers. The race was founded in 1989 by Philippe Jeantot, a French sailor and deep sea diver with a passion for adventure. The race starts and finishes in Les Sable-d'Olonne, in the Vendeé department in France, with a course along the clipper route down the Atlantic Ocean to the Cape of Good Hope, then clockwise around Antarctica, keeping Cape Leeuwin and Cape Horn to port, then back to Les Sables d'Olonne. The race runs between November and February and typically lasts between 110 to 170 days.

See: Macarthur, Ellen. *Taking on the World : A Sailor's Extraordinary Solo Race Around the Globe*. Camden, ME: International Marine Publishing, 2003. Print.

D.B. COOPER

On November 21, 1971 a man named D.B. Cooper boarded a Boeing 727 en route from Portland, Oregon to Seattle, Washington. In mid-flight the passenger told an attendant that he had a bomb and that as soon as the plane landed the authorities must give him $200,000 in cash and a set of four parachutes.

Once the plane landed and the passengers had gotten off the plane without any knowledge of Cooper's demands, the plane took off based on his instruction. Soon after being in the air Cooper leapt out of the plane into a stormy night sky with the parachutes and the cash. He was never heard from again and the stolen cash has never been used. The FBI has asserts that it believes that Cooper died in the descent or in the frigid climate.

In 2007 the F.B.I. claimed that it had obtained a partial DNA profile for D.B. Cooper and released never before seen documents, including composite sketches of the man in question. Despite the fact that the FBI believes that Cooper is dead several people have become suspects over the years. The list of suspects included the murderer John List, who in 1971 murdered his wife, mother, and three children and remained a fugitive for over seventeen years. List had stolen exactly $200,000 from his mother's bank account just prior to the skyjacking, yet when he was arrested in 1989 he denied being Cooper.

In 2007 *New York* magazine ran a story titled *Unmasking D.B. Cooper* in which the suspect is Kenneth Christiansen, a former employee of Northwest Airlines and a paratrooper. Christiansen once lived in Washington near the skyjacking and was familiar with the terrain and resembled the composite sketches. In 1972 Christiansen purchased a home for $16,500 in cash, despite the fact that he was making around

$500 a month. Christiansen died in 1994 and it was only after his death that his family became aware of nearly $400,000 in his bank account.

THE PET CEMETARY

In Ancient Egypt some animals such as cats were mummified and stored in tombs. Ancient Israeli's buried their animals in pet cemeteries. During excavation at the Ashkelon national park in Israel researchers found over 700 partial or complete dog carcasses from the fifth-century BC. Each dog carcass was carefully and individually placed in a shallow pit dug into the fill of what had previously been a warehouse.[XXIII]

The Cimetière des Chiens, which in French means "a cemetery for dogs," is the world's oldest pet cemetery. Founded in 1899 just outside Paris, France, it came about after a new law stated that people could no longer discard their dead pets in the city streets or dump them into the Seine resulting in pollution and disease.

THE HIKIKOMORI

Hikikomori is the Japanese phenomenon of withdrawing from society, or what is known as Adjustment Disorder, which involves living in almost total physical isolation. The word literally translates into "pulling away and being confined."

Though social withdrawal is not a distinctly Japanese phenomenon and there are millions of such cases around the world, in Japan the hikikomori phenomenon is considered an epidemic. The majority of hikikomori are men between the ages of 20-30, and it is estimated that there are 1-1.2 million of such cases, that's 1 out of 10 men in that particular age category.

There are several theories as to the causes for such social withdrawal, the dominating theory being that young men who have faced academic and social failures choose to withdraw from the world that did not accept them, suffering anxiety due to the strict demands for academic and financial success in Japanese society. Almost all of the hikikomori are supported by their parents. There are programs that assist hikikomori's with moving out of their parents homes into hikikomori dorms, where they learn to interact with people again and eventually find jobs.

But of course the pulling away from society is not unique to Japanese men, as Michael Zielenziger wrote in his book on the subject, *Shutting Out the Sun: How Japan Created Its Own Lost Generation*, the first widely public case of shutting oneself out from public view was with Crown Princess Masako, who since 2002 has suffered from the stressors of giving birth to an heir-son, has remained completely out of public view. Zielen-ziger points to socio-historic circumstances as an answer to this large phenomenon:

"Her [Princess Masako's] setbacks, however, also signify something deeper and more widely tragic. Sixty years after the end of World War Two, contemporary Japan is at peace, but everyone who lives there knows something is wrong. During three exhilarating decades of economic triumph Japan exercised its own unique brand of government-guided capitalism and seemed destined to outmuscle the United States, redraw the map of global influence, and take its place as the world's next superpower. Yet today its people remain afflicted with a habit of gloom, disappointment, and chronic underachievement. Like its crown princess, the nation and its young people seem to be teetering on the edge of a nervous breakdown."[XXIV]

See: Zielenziger, Michael. *Shutting out the sun: how Japan created its own lost generation*. New York: Nan A. Talese, 2006.

ANCIENT ASTRONAUTS

The ancient astronaut theory proposes that the Earth has been visited by aliens, most likely in pre-historic times, imparting science, culture, and language upon the human race.

Proponents of the theory point to religious texts, ancient artifacts, artwork, and monumental architecture as the evidence of ancient alien visitation.

The pyramids at Giza, Egypt and the Nazca Lines in Peru are often cited as being constructions by or for ancient astronauts, citing that the Nazca Lines can only be visible from the air, and that the Egyptian pyramids are too architecturally advanced to have been constructed by the ancient Egyptians.[28]

Ancient astronaut theorists cite the similarities between cultures separated by vast distances and oceans as evidence that there was a common thread of knowledge running through these civilizations, such as the construction of pyramids and depictions of strange flying vehicles, saucers, and people that appear to be wearing space-suites.

In 1898 an out-of-place artifact (see *Out-of-Place Artifacts*) was discovered in a tomb near Saqqara, Egypt that resembles an airplane and has been referred to as the Saqqara Bird. Thought it has been scientifically dated to 200 BC, it has the

---

[28] The Nazca Lines are considered to be among the most interesting and bizarre geoglyphs in the world. They are located in the Nazca Desert in Peru and are believed to have been created by the Nazca culture between 200 and 700 BC. There are hundreds of individual figures ranging from bizarre lines that appear like landing strips to visually creative representations of monkeys, fish, llamas, and other animals. The largest are over 660 feet across. To this day there is no explanation as to the meaning of the Nazca Lines. For more information see Evan Hadingham's 1988 book *Lines to the Mountain Gods: Nazca and the Mysteries of Peru.*

exact proportions of an advanced form of a pusher-glider plane, though it is missing a tailplane that would act as a stabilizer. Egyptian archeologist Khalil Messiha has argued that the tailplane went missing, but according to him it nevertheless proves that the Ancient Egyptians had developed the first aircraft. Similar depictions of what appears to be airplanes were found in pre-Columbian civilizations.

Some ancient astronaut theoreticians have pointed to the Sanskrit word *vimana*, which are sometimes described as flying machines in Sanskrit epics. For example in the great *Ramayana,* the *vimana* is called the *pushpaka*, and is described as a chariot that goes anywhere at will and resembles a bright cloud in the sky. In the *Mahabharata* the *vimana's* have the power to turn invisible and are operated via a circular reflector. Theoreticians posit that these are examples of flying space-crafts which early civilizations had witnessed and recorded.

In 1959 Soviet astrophysicist Iosif Shklovsky studied the orbital motion of Phobos, the larger and closer of the two moons orbiting Mars. Shklovsky concluded that Phobos was experiencing orbital decay, a process of prolonged reduction in the height of a satellite's orbit. Shklovsky posited that the only reason for this decay was that Phobos must be hollow. This information led some to believe that it was artificially created and perhaps done by aliens. These theories have not been supported by the mainstream academic community.

See: Daniken, Erich Von. *Chariots of the Gods?*. 7th Printing ed. United States and Canada: Bantam, 1971.

TAPHEPHOBIA

Taphephobia is the fear of being buried alive. Though today it may seem odd, history proves to us that such a fear is much warranted. Premature burials were a frightening affair and they occurred often before scientific and medical advances were made that could prove a person was indeed dead and not in a coma or in a deep sleep. There were hundreds, if not thousands, of cases of premature burials.

The signs of someone buried alive were only visible after the coffin was opened and the corpse or skeleton had obviously moved into a suffering position, as if attempting to get out, often the coffin would bare claw marks, blood stains and torn clothing.

When a person is buried a live they can live for one to two hours. If the coffin is made of light wood then a person may be able to get out, though this has occurred rarely.

Taphephobia was so prevalent in the eighteenth and nineteenth-centuries that special coffins were designed so that if a person was indeed buried alive he could pull on a chord attached to a bell above the grave. Historian Jan Bonderson writes:

"The famous German philosopher Arthur Schopenhauer freely admitted to a fear of premature interment and stipulated that his corpse rest above ground five full days before burial. The Austrian writer Johann Nepomuk Nestroy was much more elaborate in his precautions. In his will, he declared that the risk of premature burial was the only thing he feared in his present situation and that his studies of the literature on this subject had taught him that the doctors could not be relied on to distinguish dead people from living ones. His body was to be kept in an open coffin for two days, in a waiting mortuary with a signaling apparatus that would herald any signs of life. Even after burial, the coffin lid was not to be nailed shut. Russia's most famous example of the nineteenth-century fear of premature burial is the author Nikolai Gogol. In a letter to a friend he wrote that it was amazing that, as he read in a book, the human organism could exist in a state of trance for long periods of time and that the individual could see, hear, and feel, but not move, speak, or do anything to prevent being prematurely buried. In his will, Gogol specified that he not be buried until there were clear signs of petrifaction and until it was ascertained that there was no heartbeat and no peripheral pulsations. . . . When his [Gogol's] coffin was exhumed many years after his death in 1852 it was seen that the body was lying on its side; according to a German author, there was only one explanation for this: Gogol had awakened in the coffin, and a terrible struggle had occurred."[XXV]

DANDYISM

A "dandy" is a term that describes a man who gives an undue amount of attention to his manner of dress, speech, and social activity. Such a man can also be described as a "foppish ninny, a silly fellow, and a dandiner to waddle."

The term came into usage in mid-1700s Britain, and its most becoming model was George Bryan "Beau" Brummell. Brummell was perhaps the first "celebrity" as we know the term today, for he was famous simply for being a leader in man's fashion during Regency England, and is often credited as establishing the wearing of a man's suit with a tie. Oscar Wilde and Marcel Proust were good examples of dandy's, both men who gave up an exceptional amount of time on their appearance.

CONSTRUCTED LANGUAGES

In essence every language in the world is a construction; even languages which have evolved naturally over the course of thousands of years are man-made.[29] Certain languages are

---

[29] According to Abrahamic tradition the language of God is the Adamic language, one that was spoken by Adam and Eve in the Garden of Eden before Man's fall from grace. Some ancient Egyptians and Greeks believed that their language was the language of the gods

newer then others, many are linked to each other, and some are language-isolates, meaning they are not related to any other living language on the planet.

The majority of the world speaks a naturally evolved language, yet over the course of history some have invented languages, constructing them either out of a vocabulary of other existing tongues, called *posteriori language*, or constructed totally new vocabularies, which is called a *priori language*.

One of the earliest and most fascinating examples of a priori language is that of Lingua Ignota, a language invented by the twelfth-century Christian mystic Saint Hildegard.[30] Lingua Ignota, which in Latin means "unknown language," is a fascinating work comprised of twenty-three letters with a vocabulary of no more than one-thousand words, containing only nouns and just a few adjectives. It is not certain whether Saint Hildegard wanted her language to be a universal tongue or a secret.

The creation of a language to be used as a secret was common in medieval Europe, as often works of a sensitive nature

---

as well, with bizarre and often tragic attempts at trying proving that their language was indeed a God-given language.

[30] Saint Hildegard of Bingen (1098-1179) was one of the most fascinating women of the twelfth-century. Being a Christian mystic, Benedictine abesse, poet, and musician, made her one of the most dynamic figures of medieval society. Saint Hildegard wrote over eighty musical works which are performed to this day, as well as important letters, songs, poems, and books.

had to be kept from prying eyes which could jeopardize the life of the author, especially if the writings were of a sensitive and anti-establishment matter, a tradition which continued through the Renaissance into the age of Enlightenment. One such language may be contained within the mysterious Voynich Manuscript.

The text of the manuscript is completely unknown and some believe that it is completely invented, or perhaps a code, composed sometime between the fifteenth and sixteenth-century. There are supposedly six sections to the work dealing with the herbal, astronomical, biological, cosmological, pharmaceutical, and a section on recipes.[31]

The nineteenth and twentieth-centuries saw the rise of a worldwide interest in a universal language often driven by social and religious motivations. Amongst the first of such languages was Johan Martin Schleyer's Volapük, constructed between 1879 and 1880, it was a posteriori language adopted mostly from the vocabularies of English, German, and French.

In 1887 Ludwik L. Zamenhof created Esperanto, the most widely used constructed language. Esperanto is written in

---

[31] Mystery abounds as to its authorship. Some claim that the English philosopher Roger Bacon was its author; others suspect the English scientist and occultist John Dee. The manuscript is named after Wilfred Voynich, a book dealer who acquired the manuscript in 1912. Since 2005 the manuscript is housed in the Beinecke Rare Book and Manuscript Library at Yale University.

Latin characters borrowing the vocabulary of Romance and Germanic languages while using the phonology of Slavic languages.   Since it is not an official language of any state or organization (except for the International Academy of Science in San Marino), it is difficult to estimate the amount of native speakers and how many people use the language as a second language, or have a working knowledge.

Nonetheless, there have been estimates – it is believed that there are around 1 ½ million speakers (native and 2nd language) of Esperanto today.   Novels, movies, plays, poetry, and music have been written in Esperanto.

See: Richardson, David. *Esperanto Learning and Using the International Language*. 3rd ed. Newington, CT: Esperanto League For North Amer, 2004.

MOSCOW METRO-2

The Moscow Metro-2 is the unofficial name of a supposed underground rail system in Moscow not open to the public. According to various sources and conspiracy theories Metro-2 was built in the 1930s to facilitate the Soviet secret police to move quickly throughout the city without detection, and which today supposedly facilitates the transport of the FSB, the successor to the KGB. Some claim that the metro is larger than the one available to the public and that it has as many as four lines, connecting to the major arteries of the city, including FSB (former KGB) headquarters. Though there is no official evidence, and the FSB has not denied its existence, there is a group of people who have claimed to have built the Metro and others who have claimed to have physically seen it. A small subculture of young Muscovites who explore the forbidden tunnels below the city has emerged. These self-described "diggers" claim to have stumbled upon the forbidden Metro-2.

AMPHIGOURI

Amphigouri are poems composed with some humorous, whimsical, and sometimes meaningless and irrational verses, often written for children. The "nonsense poem" phenomenon began in the early 19th century with a collection of limericks titled *The Book of Nonesense* by Edward Lear. Lear wrote several nonsense books, including nonsense songs, stories, botany, and alphabets. Lewis Carroll's *Alice in Wonderland* is often considered the best work to contain nonsense rhyme. Some have argued that Carroll's 1871 poem "Jabberwocky" is the greatest nonsense poem in the English language, beginning like so:

'Twas brilig, and the slithy toves
Did gyre and gimble in the wabe;
All mimsy were the borogoves
And the mome raths outgrabe.

UNCONTACTED PEOPLE

Uncontacted peoples are tribes who have chosen to remain isolated from modern civilization, living in primitive conditions without much knowledge about the advances in technology, medicine, vaccines, natural laws, or other important advances in civilization. It has been estimated that the island of New Guinea has over forty uncontacted tribes, but due to the safety concerns anthropologists and researchers have not been able to make studies of these people.

According to a 2007 study by the Brazilian National Foundation of the Indian, Brazil is home to over sixty uncontacted tribes. One of these tribes is the Kanoe do Omere, which as of 2007 has only three people.

First discovered in 1995, the tribe currently consists of Txinamanty, a forty-two year old woman, her thirty-seven year old brother Pura, and a child born to Txinamanaty and a man from a nearby Akuntsu tribe, also a small tribe numbering only five people.[32]

A larger uncontacted tribal group in Brazil is the Kayapo people whose population in 2003 has been estimated at over five-thousand. The Kayapo, who call themselves "the ones from the water-place," live on both sides of the Zingu River on the Central Brazilian Plateau. They are hunter-gatherers tribe that is known for their intricate designs and body-modifications.

North Sentinel Island is home to the most uncontacted people on Earth. The Sentinelese are extremely hostile to intruders, modern civilization and technology, often aiming and firing arrows at boats, helicopters, and killing intruders. Though officially the island belongs to the government of Andaman and Nicobar Islands, the policy of the local government is to leave the Sentinelese in isolation since they so strongly reject contact with outsiders.

The Sentinelese's isolation makes them amongst the most mysterious peoples in the modern world since so little is known about their culture and society. The few things that are known are that they live in communal huts in small nuclear families of a mother, father, and 3-4 children. They are

---

[32] The Akuntsa tribe is rather old in age and it is believed that they will die out, since a child born to the tribe in 2000 died in a storm. These facts are last confirmed in the spring of 2011.

a hunter-gatherer society whose weaponry is made up of arrows, javelins, and flatbows. Almost nothing is known of their language. Experts estimate that there are between 100-500 Sentinelese on the island.

The Yanomani are a group of indigenous Amerindians located in areas of Venezuela and Brazil. They live in remote jungle locations and have remained cut off from the outside world, making them amongst the last few uncontacted people. The people rely completely on the jungle for their food and supplies by harvesting bananas and hunting for fish and animals. Each village lives in a communal house called the *shabano*, which is a round building with an opening in the center.

JAINISM

Jainism is an ancient religion existing primarily in the Indian peninsula, totaling some 4 million adherents. Founded in the sixth-century BC by Nataputta Mahavira – a contemporary of Buddha – Jainism was once a major rival to Buddhism.

The Jains believe that the universe is infinite, eternal, and passes through immense cycles in which souls, or *jivas*, live. These *jivas* can be everything, including inanimate objects such as rocks. Due to the laws of *karma*, *jivas* are trapped in material bodies and only through meditation, good deeds, and asceticism can the *jiva* be liberated.

The Jains place an exceptionally high value upon asceticism, and preach that even laymen who are Jains should practice strict asceticism (fasting, rituals, prayer, meditation), the goal being to become a monk. A major tenant of the religion is the philosophy of *ahimsa*, or non-violence, and strict vegetarianism and veganism is to be followed.

See: Shah, Bharat S.. *An Introduction to Jainism*. New York: BookSurge Publishing, 2002.

THE MAN IN THE IRON MASK

In a translation that appeared in the February 1895 edition of *The Chautauquan*, the popular Luxembourgian-French historian Frantz Funck-Brentano began his study with the following introduction:

"The Man with the Iron Mask! What interest, what legends, his mysterious imprisonment has given rise to! What floods of ink have been poured out in clearing up the true history of his career! Marius Topin, writing on this inexhaustible subject in 1870, stated that since the time of Voltaire no less than fifty writers had striven to untangle the threads of conjecture which had wrapped him about. And Topin had forgot at least a dozen, and did not pretend to enumerate the monographs on the subject, which are still in manuscript in our archives, nor the authors of general histories – not to mention the dramas, novels, and poems."[33][XXVI]

The Man in the Iron Mask was the name of a mysterious prisoner held in several jails throughout France during the reign of Louis XIV. The first mention of the mysterious prisoner appears in the diary of a Bastille prison warden who describes that on September 18, 1698, a certain Monsieur de Saint Mars, the former governor of Pinerolo, arrived to take charge as the governor of the infamous prison. The monsieur brought along with him a prisoner whom he always kept masked and whose name was never spoken. The prisoner was placed in the in a solemn fitted room in the tower of the prison, personally attended to by a certain Rosarges, who was apparently the major of the fortress, and fed from the governor's table.

Five years later the prisoner died and much to the curiosity of the jailers and the warden was buried in new white clothes, and everything in his room was burned and melted. The general public interest began to grow significantly after the death of the man with the mask, which as historical evidence has proven to us, was not of iron but of black cloth.

The first people in the public to begin writing on the topic were those that had contact with the prisoner, had seen him

---

[33] Marius Topin was a French historian who authored the popular 1870 study of the mystery by the title of *L'homme au masque de fer*.

personally, or had been in the vicinity. Amongst these was Palteau, the grandnephew of the governor, who gathered the eyewitness accounts of the peasants who had witnessed the governor and the prisoner when on their way to the Bastille had stopped at the governor's ancestral estate. According to the peasant's they witnessed the governor dining with his prisoner. Palteau writes:

"The peasants I questioned could not see whether or not he ate with his mask on. But they noticed that Monsieur de Saint Mars, who as opposite him, laid two pistols by the side of this plate. A single valet served them and kept the door of the room carefully closed. When the prisoner crossed the court he had on his black mask. The peasants could see his lips and teeth. He was tall, with white hair."[XXVII]

Another peasant out of sheer curiosity snuck in to watch the prisoner sleep and described him as stocky, with a white face, and though in the prime of his youth, had white hair. Other similar tales and letters appeared for some time after the death of the prisoner.

Perhaps nobody contributed more greatly to the legend of the prisoner than Voltaire. In his carefully researched and well prepared 1751 work *The Age of Louis XIV*, Voltaire begins the story in 1662 with an iron-masked prisoner on the island of Saint Margaret, who was apparently of high social stature, perhaps of the nobility, mostly due to the prisoner's interest in fine linen. While at Saint Margeret, the prisoner apparently attempted to escape by throwing a metallic plate out of his cell on which he had written some sort of message. Unfortunately for the masked prisoner the plate was picked up by an illiterate fisherman who returned it to the governor.

In 1771 Voltaire evolved his story of the mysterious prisoner, and theorized that he was the half-brother of Louis XIV, and that once the monarch discovered the truth imprisoned him. In 1790 the Duc de Richelieu claimed that the governor had stated that the prisoner was the twin of Louis XIV. But it was Alexandre Dumas' brilliant novel 1847-1850 serial *The Vicomte of Bragelonne: Ten Years Later* that had brought the mystery of the masked prisoner to the general public. Brooklyn College Professor Natasha Pogrebinsky has suggested that because of the mysterious prisoner's youth, supposed white hair and pale skin that he might have been afflicted with albinism. The fact that he was treated with extreme caution and even respect suggests that he was of royal or wealthy stock and thus kept in what was essentially an eighteenth-century version of a twentieth-century prison hospital.

THE PILLAR SAINTS

Saint Simeon Stylites was a Christian ascetic who is best remembered for sitting atop a column for most of his life as a form of penance.[34] Born in Syria in 390, Simeon became a devoted Christian in his early years, apparently after hearing the Beatitudes and deciding to follow a path of austerity.

While still a teenager Simeon entered a monastery where he devised extreme methods of torturing himself, he would eat only once a week and give the rest of the food to the poor; he would sleep standing up so that he would only be able to have a few moments of rest and devote everything else to prayer. At one point he tied a rope so tightly around his body that it went through the skin; eventually the skin grew over the rope. The rope bondage resulted in an infection and the young Simeon almost died.

His austerities eventually proved too trying for the monastic community and he left them only to experiment with much

---

[34] The term *stylite* derives from the word *stylos*, meaning "pillar." On an interesting side note: pole-sitting was an American fad from 1924 to 1929 where people would sit atop flag poles for as long as they could in an attempt to beat records. It started when Alvin "Shipwreck" Kelly sat on a flagpole for 13 hours and 13 minutes; similar feats were attempted by others soon afterward. As of 2011 the world record for pole-sitting is held by Daniel Baraniuk from Poland who sat on an 8-foot pole for 196 days from May 15 to November 26, 2002

harsher methods of mortification and asceticism. At one point he tied himself to a rock with a chain and lived in a hole in the ground. Soon people began making pilgrimages towards the ascetic. Trying to flee people once more he climbed a pillar, as there were many pillars at this time in Syria due to hundreds of years of Roman rule. As more crowds came to learn from the ascetic, the column grew larger. Eventually it is believed the column reached the height of sixty feet.

Theodoret the Bishop of Cyrrhus wrote of seeing Simeon atop the column:

"I myself admire his patient endurance. For night and day he stands in open view. He had the doors taken away and a good part of the enclosing wall destroyed, and so presents to everyone a new and extraordinary spectacle: sometimes he stands for a long time; sometimes he bends over many times and offers worship to God. Many of the bystanders attempted to count these prostrations. Once one of my attendants counted one thousand, two hundred and forty-four, but then was distracted and lost count."

Simeon spent thirty-seven years atop the pillar, dying at the age of sixty-nine in 459. A church was built surrounding the column, which though in ruins stands to this day. Simeon lived life atop the column influencing several generations of pillar saints, or *stylites*.

Perhaps the most interesting pillar saint other than Simeon was Daniel the Stylite who was born in 409 in Syria and admitted to a monastery at an early age. While on a trip with an abbot to Antioch the two stopped near Simeon's pillar where the young Daniel was blessed by the famous pillar saint.

At the age of forty-two Daniel had a vision in which Simeon directed him to mount a *stylos* and live his life in imitation of the older pillar saint. Daniel had a pillar erected on the borders of Constantinople and, wearing Simeon's ragged tunic, he mounted it. From then on he lived atop the pillar for the next forty-one years. On that column near Constantinople he was ordained by St. Gennadius, preached sermons, and supposedly cured the sick and experienced prophetic visions. He soon became an attraction, and gave council to the Emperors Leo and Zeno and the Patriarch of Constantinople.

There was another Simeon Stylites as well, who is remembered by the church as Saint Simeon Stylites the Younger. He was born in 521 at Antioch, not far from the pillar of the first Simeon. Feeling a calling towards a life of prayer and meditation it is said that he had climbed his first pillar at such a young age that he lost his first teeth upon the *stylos*, upon which he lived for over sixty years.

The seventh-century Saint Alypius the Stylite from Hadrianopolis lived atop a pillar for most of his life, dying at the age of one-hundred and eight.

See: *The Lives of Simeon Stylites (Cistercian Studies)*. Kalamazoo: Cistercian Publications, 1989.

THE ANARCHIST COOKBOOK

The Anarchist Cookbook is a 160-page book first published in 1971 with recipes for the manufacturing of explosives, telephone freaking (*hacking*), and other dangerous activity for the purpose of undermining political institutions and powers. In 2011 the popular website *The Daily Beast* wrote:

"Published in 1971, it would sell more than 2 million copies worldwide and influence dozens of malcontents, mischief-makers, and killers. Police have linked it to the Croatian radicals who bombed Grand Central Terminal and hijacked a TWO flight in 1976; the Puerto Rican separatists who bombed FBI headquarters in 1981; Thomas Spinks, who led a group that bombed at least 10 American abortion clinics in the mid-1980s; and the 2005 London public-transport bombers."[XXVIII]

The author of the book is William Powell, who wrote it when he was just nineteen years old, and who in the context of the Vietnam War and the looming danger of a draft into that war, composed it as a symbol of protest. Powell wrote the manual using declassified army manuals in the New York Public Library, and had no personal real-life experience in making any of the deadly explosives.

According to the FBI, soon after the publication of the manual bombings went up dramatically in the United States. But Powell soon rescinded his support for his book, and dropped out of the radical scene, devoting himself to education. Throughout the 1970s and 1980s Powell worked as an educator, earning a master's degree, getting married, and traveling the world teaching at private schools set up by the State Department. In many ways he had forgotten about his past.

But with the advent of the internet in the 1990s, and the spread of his work throughout the web, Powell came under scrutiny for his past publication and even had to resign from a school in Tanzania as a result.

Then Powell went on the "offensive" and began to include the book in his resume, as well as posting the following message on the Amazon.com page for his publication:

"The Anarchist Cookbook was written during 1968 and part of 1969 soon after I graduated from high school. At the time, I was 19 years old and the Vietnam War and the so-called "counter culture movement" were at their height. I was involved in the anti-war movement and attended numerous peace rallies and demonstrations. The book, in many respects, was a misguided product of my adolescent anger at the prospect of being drafted and sent to Vietnam to fight in a war that I did not believe in.

I conducted the research for the manuscript on my own, primarily at the New York City Public Library. Most of the contents were gleaned from Military and Special Forces Manuals. I was not member of any radical group of either a left or right wing persuasion.

I submitted the manuscript directly to a number of publishers without the help or advice of an agent. Ultimately, it was accepted by Lyle Stuart Inc. and was published verbatim - without editing - in early 1970. Contrary to what is the normal custom, the copyright for the book was taken out in the name of the publisher rather than the author. I did not appreciate the significance of this at the time and would only come to understand it some years later when I requested that the book be taken out of print.

The central idea to the book was that violence is an acceptable means to bring about political change. I no longer agree with this.

. . .

During the years that followed its publication, I went to university, married, became a father and a teacher of adolescents. These developments had a profound moral and spiritual effect on me. I found that I no longer agreed with what I had written earlier and I was becoming increasingly uncomfortable with the ideas that I had put my name to. In 1976 I became a confirmed Anglican Christian and shortly thereafter I wrote to Lyle Stuart Inc. explaining that I no longer held the views that were expressed in the book and requested that The Anarchist

Cookbook be taken out of print. The response from the publisher was that the copyright was in his name and therefore such a decision was his to make - not the author's. In the early 1980's, the rights for the book were sold to another publisher. I have had no contact with that publisher (other than to request that the book be taken out of print) and I receive no royalties.

Unfortunately, the book continues to be in print and with the advent of the Internet several websites dealing with it have emerged. I want to state categorically that I am not in agreement with the contents of The Anarchist Cookbook and I would be very pleased (and relieved) to see its publication discontinued. I consider it to be a misguided and potentially dangerous publication which should be taken out of print."[XXIX]

See: Powell, William. *The Anarchist Cookbook*. New York City: Ozark Press, Llc, 2003.

STRUCK BY LIGHTENING

Roy Cleveland Sullivan of the United States is perhaps the only person to have been struck by lightning seven times. His first lightning strike occurred in 1942 when he was in a lookout tower; he lost a nail on his big toe. The second strike occurred in 1969 while he was driving a car, this time he was knocked unconscious and his eyebrows got burned. The third occurred in 1970, while working in his front yard. The fourth in 1972, while in a ranger station, setting his hair on fire. In 1973 a lightning bolt hit him in the head, setting his head on fire again. In 1974 he was struck for the sixth time, while camping. In 1977 he was hit for the seventh time, while he was fishing. It is unknown if he has been struck since 1977. He died in 1983 from natural causes.

DIVINATION

Dowsing, or "water witching," is an occult practice of using a forked implement to find sources of water, minerals, treasure, other humans, or whatever is desired by the dowser. The practice seems to have become popular during the European Middle Ages and has often been attributed to paganism and witchcraft.

In the twentieth-century there have been many studies that conclude there is no scientific basis for the practice of dowsing, and that though sometimes the dowsers did reach sources of water, they were just as likely to find these sources by chance. Nevertheless, the act is still popular in folk magic, ritual, and there even exist several modern dowsing societies such as the American Society of Dowsers founded in 1961.

Dowsing is part of a larger paranormal or parapsychological realm known as divination, which is a ritualistic attempt at gaining insight into the make-up of things, situations, or of being able to see-through or uncover what is hidden and not open to average human beings. In the twentieth-century a form of divination called *radiesthesia* – the ability to detect radiation within the human body without scientific means – entered the English language.

In 1953, UNESCO sponsored a committee of prominent European scientists in their study of radioesthiesa. Their carefully considered consensus was that "there can be no doubt that it is a fact." The Academie des Sciences of Paris has commented that "it is impossible to deny the existence of the power, although its nature cannot be determined." Five Nobel Prize winners have endorsed dowsing, and so has the Institute of Technical Physics of the Dutch National Research Council.[xxx]

MAUNSELL FORTS

The Maunsell Sea Forts are fortified towers built in the Thames Estuary and the River Mercy by Great Britain during the Second World War. They were built in order to report German air raids and were operated by the Royal Navy. Some were built in international waters and were completely decommissioned in the 1950s.

Throughout the 1960s the forts were used to transmit pirate radio. Rough Sands Fort has become the most famous of the fortified towers. It was occupied by Paddy Roy Bates (1922-

) in the early 1960s from where he transmitted his pirate radio station "Britain's Better Music Station." In 1964 he declared the fort a sovereign country, or a micronation, called the Principality of Sealand. Sealand has never been officially recognized by any government, yet it is also not claimed by any government and since Sealand is located in international waters it is in essence a sovereign state.

Paddy Roy Bates has fought off several "invaders" to the small principality, including the British navy and pirates with whom he has had gun battles. At one point a few Dutchmen and a German attempted to seize Sealand in the late 1970s, in the end Bates captured them and held them as prisoners of war, until finally reaching a compromise with Dutch and German diplomats and releasing the men unharmed. Sealand has its own flag, coins, stamps, and noble titles which can be purchased for £29.99. In recent years, as micronations become a bizarrely popular internet fad, Sealand has garnered international attention and has been the subject of television documentaries and stories in the media.

MYSTICAL STIGMATA

Stigmata are wounds which appear on the body of exceptionally devout Christians corresponding with the wounds on Jesus Christ's body during the crucifixion, specifically on the palms and joints of the hands, feet, and the upper body.[35] Stigmatics are almost always ecstatic's, people who experience trances, visions, and whose minds are given to moments of ecstasy in which the worldly senses are suspended and one experiences a sense of transcendence, awe, or fear.

The phenomenon traces its historical roots to the thirteenth-century, with St. Francis of Assisi, who received his first stigmata in 1224, just two years before his death, after experiencing a vision during the Feast of the Cross, a feast which commemorates the crucifixion of Christ. While Francis was praying, and experiencing the vision of a seraph with six wings and hands extended, and attempted to comprehend this vision, wounds began to appear on his hands and feet, seemingly pierced by nails. In 1230 Thomas of Celano wrote:

"His hands and feet seemed to be pierced through the middle by nails, whose heads appeared in the inner sides of the hands and on the upper sides of the feet and their pointed ends on the opposite sides. The marks in the hands were round on the inner side, but on the other side they were elongated; and some small pieces of flesh took on the appearance of the ends

---

[35] Stigmata derives from the Latin *stigma*, meaning "mark or brand made onto the skin with a hot iron," or simply, to "puncture." It can therefore be translated as simply bearing the brand of Jesus Christ. Prior to the 1600s this term was mostly used as to describe brands on slaves, or brands of shame or disgrace, but has since been applied almost exclusively to seriously devout Christians who experience these supernatural marks.

of the nails, bent and driven back and rising above the rest of the flesh. In the same way the marks of the nails were impressed upon the feet and raised in a similar way above the flesh. Furthermore, his right side was as though it had been pierced by the lance and had a wound, which frequently bled and covered his tunic and trousers with his sacred blood. He made every effort to conceal this miracle from both friars and those outside the order."[36] XXXI

Though Francis attempted to hide his marks, they were witnessed by several friars, monks, and lay people during his lifetime. These marks seemed to not go away, and remained even after his death two years later. The significance of his stigmata had much to do with the supposed miracles that were accompanied in relation to the stigmata, such as the appearance of his stigmatic wounds on images depicting him, and his tomb having the miraculous ability to heal others of their wounds, diseases, and ailments.

St. Francis was thus amongst the first Christians to be considered a martyr not having perished a typical martyr's life, that is being killed for his belief, but a martyr in the sense of living his life in a state of penance and suffering, bearing open wounds. St. Francis was the first documented stigmatic, and

---

[36] Thomas of Celano (c.1185-c.1220) was a Franciscan friar and contemporary of Francis, hailed from the small town of Celano in the Abruzzi region, entering the Order in 1214. He was the first hagiographer of Francis.

though it is considered a miracle, it was obviously one that gave him – and would give others in the future – a great amount of paint and shame.

Since the thirteenth-century over three-hundred Christian mystics and ecstatics have had definite recorded stigmata's. Over sixty saints of both sexes had this experience, including the co-patron saint of Italy Catherine of Sienna. This phenomenon, though medieval in origin, has continued into the twenty-first century. The most notable twentieth-century stigmatic was the Italian priest Padre Pio (1887-1968), who from 1918 until his death in 1968 experienced the stigmata on his hands.

The scientific community has attempted to explain this phenomenon. Medical officials who have examined ecstatic do not claim that the wounds are not genuine, yet they cannot prove that they are supernatural. Some have posited that the ecstatics create these wounds during their ecstatic or hysterical experiences, where they may not be aware that they are mutilating themselves while in a dissociative state.

LINGUISTIC RELATIVITY

Linguistic relativity, or the Sapir-Whorf hypothesis, is the theory that the way a person understands the world is dependent on the language that they speak. With over 5,000 languages in existence, many of which do not belong to the same language-family, this theory postulates that the differences in language results in differences in cognitive experiences.

Linguists such as Noam Chomsky hold that languages embody specific worldviews, therefore each language or language-family embody different views. Proponents of this concept often point to the Hanunoo, who have over 90 names for rice, thus transferring a different reality.

Several linguists and writers have constructed their own languages in order to further explore the Sapir-Whorf hypothesis. In 1955 sociologist James Cooke Brown constructed Loglan, partially to test the hypothesis, as well as create a new international language, but also to see if people would think differently if learning this language. Loglan is structured around logic, and therefore considered an early form of an engineered language, which are based predicate logic.

In 1982 American science fiction author and linguist Suzette Haden Elgin created Láadan, a language which was designed to express the perceptions of a human woman and to see if this language would be able to shape a culture. Láadan implies that existing human languages are inadequate in that they do not express the perceptions of women, but are rather male-centric, that women are forced to speak in methods appropriate for men, rather than expressing directly how they feel.[37] Thus if women had a language which better expressed

---

[37] Nüshu is the only exclusively-female language in the world, originating in feudal China in the Xiaoshui Valley in Jiangyong County,

their perceptions then it might be possible to reflect a different reality. The language was included in her first novel, *Native Tongue*. Writing in 1999 on her website, Elgin wrote of the experiment:

"The results of this experiment were clear. For the first three hypotheses being tested – that the weak form of the linguistic relativity hypothesis is true, that Goedel's Theorem applies to language, and that change in language brings about social change – I ended up with nothing more than anecdotal information. The fourth hypothesis – that if women were offered a women's language they would either welcome and nurture it or would replace it with a better one – was proved false. (It was of course almost inevitable that if the fourth hypothesis failed I would learn nothing much about the other three, since they only begin to be tested if the fourth one succeeds).

"As I said . . . interesting. It was well worth the effort. Whether results would have been different if I'd given the experiment twenty years instead of ten, or if Star Trek had decided to present episodes about a war between a Láadan-speaking population and the Kingons, or any of a multitude of other modifications in conditions, is impossible to say;

Hunan Province. It is a secret language used only amongst females and has evolved on its own as male society paid no attention to the activities of women. Unlike written Chinese which is logographic, Nüshu is phonetic, using between 400-700 characters representing a syllable.

whether something different will happen when the reprint edition of *Native Tongue* comes out form Feminist Press is impossible tos ay. Experiments have to have limits ore they have no scientific value. . . . Meanwhile, the Klingon language thrives – from which you are free to draw your own conclusions."[XXXII]

See: Leavitt, John. *Linguistic Relativities: Linguistic Diversity and Modern Thought*. New York: Cambridge University Press, 2011.

MCMURDO STATION

McMurdo Station is the largest research station on the southern tip of Ross Island in Antarctica operated by the United States Antarctic Program. The station supports over 1,000 researchers throughout the summers and over 200 in the winters. It is Antarctica's largest community, with internet and satellite connections, over 100 buildings, a research science center, 3 airfields, an ATM, a spa, a coffee shop, two bars, and a church.[38]

Most of the day to day functions are operated by defense contractors. Every year cargo ships deliver over eight million gallons of fuel and eleven million pounds of supplies and equipment for the station. Building 155 houses the cafeteria,

---

[38] The Chapel of the Snows is a small interfaith Christian church and the world's most southern religions building. It is capable of holding up to 63 people per service.

dorm rooms, and a store that sells snack foods, drinks, souvenirs, and essentials such as toothpaste, soap, and shampoo. There is also a television station, AFAN-TV, which runs vintage programs. McMurdo also has access to the internet as well as voice and satellite communications.

See: Legler, Gretchen. *On the Ice: An Intimate Portrait of Life at McMurdo Station, Antarctica (World As Home, The)*. Minneapolis: Milkweed Editions, 2005.

PROLIFIC AUTHORS

The Brazilian writer Jose Carlos Ryoki de Alpiom Inoe, who writes under the name Ryoki Inoue as well as thirty-nine other pseudonyms, has been acknowledged as the world's most prolific author with over 1,083 original novels, novellas, and epics in print.

Born in 1946 to a Japanese father and a Portuguese mother in São Paulo, Ryoki studied medicine and worked as a doctor through the 1970s and 1980s, until in 1986 he began writing pulp fiction with an incredible output, producing new novels within twenty-four hour periods. Between 1986 and 1999 Inoue had written 999 pulp fiction works, most of which dealt with cowboys, gangsters, and spies. Inoue continues to write to this day, and has a large following in Brazil and Japan.

Perhaps the only author to compete with Inoue's extraordinary output was Kathleen Lindsay. Born in 1903 in the small town of Aldershot, Hampshire, England, she received a private education at the Convent of Sacré Coeur, Paris and the Sakkakini Convent in Cairo, Egypt, Lindsay wrote under various pseudonyms, averaging four books a year.

The popular Russian-born American science-fiction writer Isaac Asimov published over 500 titles, including over 100 science-fiction anthologies, books on history, science, and literature. The Belgium author Georges Simenon wrote over 500 novels, many about the French police detective Jules Maigret.

The English-born writer Robert Payne wrote over 100 books, including long novels, deeply researched scholarly books on various historical topics, and translations of fiction and poetry from Russian, Greek, Arabic, and Chinese.

THE HANGOVER AND THE BODY

Due to dehydration the throat and mouth feel dry and scratchy, the muscles become weak, and the brain pulls from its lining, intensifying the headache caused by the dilated blood vessels. The liver builds up fatty and lactic acid resulting in low blood sugar. The stomach lining becomes inflamed and delays digestion, leading to the feeling of nausea. The kidneys do not absorb proper amounts of water, and the pancreas increases its production of digestive chemicals, leading to the sensation of pain, nausea, and inducing vomiting.

HOBO SIGN SYSTEM

Starting in the late 1800s penniless vagabonds and migratory workers, often called hobos, who travelled across the United States looking for whatever work they could find began to devise a distinct system of symbols in order to communicate with each other. Most of these symbols related to the location, direction, and population of a specific place, such as where one could get food, if the surrounded area was friendly to hobos, and if there was any work in a certain direction.

This sign system became exceedingly pronounced during the Great Depression, when the number of migratory workers increased due to the economic collapse, and the need for communication was met by the inventive and complex sign system which hoboes made with chalk, paints, or coals painted under bridges, on sidewalks, posts, doors, and fences. Some of the symbolism remains to be used; however at its peak in the 1930s millions of people could read and understand what the symbols meant.

ENDANGERED LANGUAGES

According to Ethnologue, an organization specializing in studying lesser-known languages, there are 473 endangered languages in the world as of 2010.[39]

A language assumes the status of endangered when the only people who speak it are the elderly who do not pass the language to the younger population. As long as the language is taught as a first-language and is passed on from the old generation to the young then it is considered a living language, thus even a population of fifteen-thousand speaking a distinct language can be considered living and not endangered, while two million people can speak a language that will never be passed on qualifies as endangered.

Over 150 Pacific languages are nearly extinct. In Micronesia the Nguluwan language has just fifty surviving speakers, while the Zire language in the Melanesian sub region New

---

[39] *Ethnologue* is a publication of SIL International, an American Christian nonprofit whose main goal is to serve "language communities as they build capacity for sustainable language development." Since 1934 the organization has documented, analyzed, and codified thousands of languages, many of which are limited to only a few speakers and which have become extinct. The group is controversial because it is a Christian organization that operates predominantly within non-Christian and non-Western communities, and has been accused of doing missionary work by its critics.

Caledonia has only four surviving speakers according to a 1996 census.

Most of the Oceanic languages that are going extinct have as little as one to one-hundred speakers, all elderly, who never passed on the language to their children or grandchildren. This process is known as language death, which occurs when another language enters the community, making the speakers bilingual, with one language dominating over the other, decreasing its relevance and usage, until the only remaining speakers are the elderly and no one is teaching it to the new generation. Languages that are nearly extinct are often declared dead while some of these elderly speakers are still live when it is obvious that the language will not be revived.

Over 180 languages in the Americas are on the verge of extinction. In Canada and the United States the Native-American Han language spoken in Eagle, Alaska and Dawson City, Yukon is believed to only have ten surviving speakers, all of them elderly, and the language is believed to die with these last speakers. Some of these are language isolates, meaning they are natural languages that evolved out of that distinct geographical area and bare absolutely no relation to any other language family, making them unique.

Pirahã is a dying language spoken by at least 250 indigenous Pirahã people along the Maici River in the Amazon. It is the last living language in the Muran family and is a language-isolate. Pirahã possesses an incredibly complex array of tones, syllable lengths and stresses that can only be spoken in whistles.

The fascinating Kutenai (also spelled Kootenay) language which is spoken by as little as twelve people in parts of Idaho, Montana, and British Columbia is also a language-isolate. Some linguists have hypothesized that it is related to the Salishan family of languages, but this has yet to be proven.

The Coeur d'Alene language of the Coeur d'Alene Tribe that lives at the Coeur d'Alene Reservation in Idaho has only five speakers out of a population of eight-hundred. It is believed that there are only eight to ten speakers of the Kawaiisu language spoken by the Kawaiisu people of California.

The continent of Africa has forty-six endangered languages, and has perhaps the most speakers when compared to endangered languages of all other groups and continents. The Shabo language has over six-hundred speakers in southwestern Ethiopia and the Anfillo language of western Ethiopia has at least five-hundred speakers.

As of 2002 the Karone language of Senegal and Gambia, belonging to the Niger-Congo language family, is perhaps the largest endangered language, with over ten-thousand speakers according to UNESCO.

Ethnologue and UNESCO report that there are eight nearly extinct languages of Europe. In Greece the language known as Romano-Greek (or sometimes Para-Romani) is believed to be spoken by at least thirty people, all by the Romani people, who are commonly referred to as *gypsies* in English. The language evolved by mixing Greek with Romani and was structured upon the Greek language.

The Livonian language once-spoken in Latvia lost its last native-speaker in 2003, Edgar Vaalgamaa who was born in 1918. Today there are no native speakers of the language, yet it is believed that there are at least twenty second-language speakers who took the time to learn it on their own.

Manx, the Goidelic language that was once spoken on the Isle of Man, became extinct in 1974 when its last surviving native speaker Ned Maddrell died. The language was revived however, and as of 2001 it is estimated that over one-thousand people have a competent understanding of it, learning it as a second-language.

The Vilamovian language spoken almost exclusively in the small Polish town of Wilamowice has seventy surviving speakers. For many years almost everyone in the town spoke the language and the Austro-Hungarian civil servant Florian Biesik (1849-1931) wrote poetry and set the literary standard for the tongue. After the Second World War the communist authorities forbade the language, urging the younger population to speak Polish, and thus the language began to slowly die. It is believed that the language will die out completely with the deaths of the last speakers.

The Uralic language known as the Votic language is spoken by as few as twenty citizens in the small villages of Krakolye and Luzhitsy in the Kingisepp town in the Leningrad Oblast, Russia. Between 1926 and 1959 the Vote population declined by 90%, greatly affecting the language, and many Votes identified with Russian language and culture losing their own.

See: Grimes, Barbara F., and Joseph Evans Grimes. *Ethnologue*. 14th ed. Dallas, Tex.: SIL International, 2000.

THE GATE OF HELL

The Gate of Hell, or Darvaza, is a giant gaping hole near Darvaz, Turkmenistan filled with burning natural gas. In the late 1960s the area was known for its large amount of natural gas and in 1971 geologists headed to the area to begin drilling.

Without knowledge that they were drilling over an underground cavern, the rig collapsed along with all the equipment into the massive hole. Since it was filled with deadly gasses no one could go inside the hole to retrieve the rig, the geologists decided to burn up all the gas by igniting it, thinking it will burn out in a few days. It has been burning ever since.

ABRACADABRA

Abracadabra is an ancient Semitic incantation used to cure ailments, including fevers and inflammations. The person suffering from an ailment was to wear an amulet for nine days with the written word in an inverted cone upon the amulet, below is an example in the Latin:

A - B - R - A - C - A - D - A - B - R - A
A - B - R - A - C - A - D - A - B - R
A - B - R - A - C - A - D - A - B
A - B - R - A - C - A - D - A
A - B - R - A - C - A - D
A - B - R - A - C - A
A - B - R - A - C
A - B - R - A
A - B - R
A - B
A

Its origins are mysterious; however it shares a resemblance with the Hebrew word *ha-brachah* meaning "curse" with the Aramaic *dabra* meaning "pestilence" added to the end, therefore making it *ha-bra-cha-da-bra*, a "curse for pestilence." Others have argued that the word derives from the Aramaic *ab-hadda kedhabrha* which translates into "to disappear like this word," therefore a treatment for illness. Today abracadabra is used as an almost none-sense-word by stage magicians and performers.

STRAIGHT EDGE

Straight Edge refers to a subculture within the hardcore punk music scene. The principle ethics of the subculture are that its adherents abstain from the use of alcohol, tobacco, drugs, and recreational sex. The term was coined in the 1980s by the Washington D.C. hardcore punk band Minor Threat, whose core tenants were taken from the lyrics of a song called "Straight Edge," whose central message was that the hero had better things to do then drugs and sex. Ian MacKaye, leader of the band and author of many of the songs, who does live a life of abstinence, is however not an exponent of Straight Edge as a group or subculture.

The movement has branched into two major schools – regular straight edge and Hardline. Hardline is a much more rigorous, extreme, and ascetic school, with fundamental Islamic overtones, and a strict vegan and pro-life philosophy.

Straight Edge is primarily a movement whose adherents are composed of white middle and working class teenagers; however there are many who are much older, and there are some who are of other ethnicities.

The symbol for straight edge is a capital *X,* often tattooed or drawn on the hands to signify their resistance to drugs and carnal temptation. The origin of the symbol comes from the common practice of bouncers and ticket-sellers at punk shows to draw a large X on the hands of underage customers so that they could not order beer. Soon this was adopted by even over-age customers as a symbol of solidarity and as a method of identifying themselves with a drug-free lifestyle. Sometimes the X is expanded into XXX. Straight edge is often written as "sXe" to signify the subculture, and teenage adherents will often place an x before and after their username on internet forums, e-mails, and chat's, such as: xstraightedgex.

Many straight edge people exhibit tattoos that identify themselves to the world and other straight-edgers. Common tattoos are of slogans such as "Drug Free for Life" and "True Till Death" signifying their lifelong commitment to the ideals.

The subculture is judgmental of members who drop out or "lose their edge," and are as equally judgmental of everyday people who choose to drink, smoke, and engage in casual sex, sometimes even becoming violent. In the 1990s several members of straight edge were arrested for engaging in violence against people who were smokers and drinkers, one being charged for murder.

In some parts of the United States straight edge is considered a gang, despite the fact that the majority of their members are nonviolent. October 17 is considered "National Edge

Day," a straight edge holiday in which members of the community attend local hardcore punk shows. Some members of straight edge are involved in other political and social organizations and programs that fit into the abstinence philosophy, such as organizations against drinking, animal cruelty, and pro-life issues.

See: Sober Living for the Revolution: Hardcore Punk, Straight Edge, and Radical Politics. Pennsylvania: Pm Press, 2010.

FREETOWN CHRISTIANIA

Christiania is a neighborhood in Copenhagen, Denmark which claims to be an autonomous zone, or a micronation.

The area was a military barracks dating back to the 1600s, and was later an ammunition depot until it was abandoned in the early 1970s. Soon a group of people broke down the abandoned fences and claimed Christiania a "self-governing society."

There were almost no rules, and the residents of the zone adhered to principles usually espoused by hippies, anarchists, squatters, and the like. Until 2004 when Denmark passed legislations against Christiania's supposed autonomy, the zone was known for its selling of drugs, particularly hash and marijuana. It was also a place for gangs, where several murders and rapes had taken place.

Since Christiania and its residents advocate an extremely anarchic approach to rule and society several problematic issues have arisen amongst its residents, including the issue of ownership of cars. For a long period no private property was allowed in Christiania, therefore residents who owned their own cars had to park them outside of the zone.

KUNDALINI

In yoga *Kundalini* is a dormant mystical force and energy which may be awakened through the exercise of asceticism, *pranayama* (yogic breath exercise), deep meditation, and other mystical and esoteric practices.

Some have described kundalini as a fiery serpent which lays dormant in the chakras along the spinal cord; when awakened the sensations of fire, warmth, radiance, pain, and the swelling of the spine can be felt.[40] It is believed that kundalini is

---

[40] Chakra is derived from the Sanskrit word *cakram* (चक्र), which can mean "circle," "turning," "wheel," or "disk." In Hinduism, as well as various esoteric, occult, and mystical belief-systems, chakras are believed to be energy centers which reside along the spinal cord. Each chakra can release, or open, certain energies which may reflect a change in person's physical, mental, and spiritual characteristics. They are often depicted and written about as petal-like appendages, as well as possessing a distinct color. There are seven primary chakras. The base chakra, the muladhara, is red with four petals, and is the

extremely powerful and if not awakened with the guide of a spiritual teacher can lead to physical and mental deterioration.

Kundalini is believed to exist within the *muladhara* ("root") chakra, the first of seven chakras, located at the base of the spine. The kundalini is coiled around the spine three and half times, each coil being the representation of a guṇa, or a transcending thread or tendency associated with creation, preservation, and destruction.

It is posited that as the practitioner awakens kundalini through various meditations and practices the chakras are opened; with the opening of each chakra the energy becomes greater, stronger, and moves upwards towards the next chakra.

Each chakra possesses its own specific positive and negative energy and force, and the practitioner may experience the feelings of joy, bliss, and happiness, but may also experience the sensations of depression and madness. For these awakenings the practitioner must prepare oneself to be able to understand these sensations and not fall victim to the new experiences. As the kundalini moves upward, it finally reaches the seventh and highest chakra, the *sahasrara*, located at the top

---

seat of kundalini awakening. For more information on chakras see Johari, Harish. *Chakras.* Rochester, Vt.: Destiny Books, 1987.

of the head, and the practitioner achieves some of the highest and most sought-after mystical experiences.

Proponents of kundalini argue that there are closed off and unconscious paths within our nervous system that can only be opened through varying practices, and that there are still many aspects of our body with which modern medicine and science is not familiar with, therefore the concept of kundalini should not be brushed off as mythic or bogus.

Recently there have been scientific studies conducted on deep meditation and some scientists have linked the experiences of people who claimed to have undergone kundalini with people who have survived near-deaths or have practiced intense meditation. Scientists have termed these experiences as the Kundalini Syndrome, a set of sensory, motor, mental and affective symptoms.

Most often people feel a sense of detachment from their bodies, hear strange inner noises or feel inner colors and varying temperatures in their bodies; thoughts become distorted, the body begins to move on its own without the owners commands, there is unusual breathing or paralysis, as well as out of body experiences and psychic perceptions.

In 1981 at the age of fifty-three Dorothy Walters, a professor of English and women's studies experienced what she has called an intense and spontaneous kundalini awakening. Walters describes her experience:

"The year was 1981. I was sitting in my living room on an elm-lined street in Kansas, reading a book that made passing reference to a phenomenon I had heard of but knew almost nothing about. The phenomenon was named Kundalini, said to be a "snake" that resided at the base of the spine and whose journey upward – instigated through the practice of ancient yogic techniques – would lead, ultimately, to the opening of the crown and even enlightenment. I decided to give it a try . . . I sat quietly in my chair and breathed deeply, focusing on an image of the god and goddess in union in the volume I had been reading. Suddenly I felt a ball of rapturous energy in my lower abdomen. And then, within seconds it seemed, these energies rushed upward into my head.

"I felt an influx of ecstatic energy streaming into my skull while my very brain was infused with rapture. As my crown opened, it felt like "a thousand petals unfolding," just as the ancient texts describe. The experience lasted for several minutes, and, as long as I did not think about what was happening, it continued. Suddenly I realized that I was not, in fact, a separate, autonomous, self-individuated being, but merely a tiny spark in a great, indescribable, inscrutable force, the unnamed source of all that is, that which animates and powers the universe in overwhelming love. I was fiction I told myself, a myth I had invented . . ."[XXXIII]

See: Khalsa, Dharam Singh, and Darryl O'Keeffe. *The Kundalini Yoga Experience: Bringing Body, Mind, and Spirit Together*. New York: Fireside, 2002.

LOLITA FASHION

Lolita fashion refers to a Japanese subculture (*rorrita fass-hon*) that began in the 1970s where women wear Victorian and Rococo-era clothing mixed with modern gothic elements.

This subculture is often on display at Tokyo's Harijuku neighborhood, where teenage girls are seen wearing a variety of Lolita fashions, such as Gothic Lolita, Sweet Lolita, Classic Lolita, and Punk Lolita amongst others. The fashion aims to make the teenager and some women in their 20s and 30s look like dolls or even very young children. Though the name is an obvious reference to Vladimir Nabokov's 1955 novel about an older man's relationship with a 12-year-old girl, many within the subculture claim the style is not overtly sexual and aims for cuteness rather than sex-appeal.

POUSTINIA

The *poustinia* is a term used in Russian Orthodox monasticism which literally means "desert" is a small spartan cabin where one goes to pray, confess, fast, and meditate on the nature of God.

The *poustnik* (the one who undertakes to live in a *poustinia*) is devoted to prayer and silence, however differs from a hermit in that the *poustnik* is a part of the community and makes himself available to humanity through advice and prayer.

The concept of a *poustinia* is not new for the Russian village, and it was not uncommon for men to venture to the *poustinia* and live as a *poustnik* for long periods of time or for the rest of their lives. The *poustinia* is a symbol for the thirst for spiritual silence and oneness with God, for the goal is to enter into the desert of the heart and be one with God. In the 1970s, the Catholic Catherine Doherty introduced the concept to Westerners with her book, *Poustinia: Encountering God, Silence, Solitude and Prayer.*

Jean Stairs has described it:

"A poustinia is a place of quiet and solitude which people choose to enter with a spirit of anticipation for meeting the God who dwells within them. The Russian term literally means "desert," but it means much more than arid, geographical isolation. It is less desert and more oases. It can refer to a room, a sanctuary, or a chair that one identifies as the place reserved for entering the quiet room of one's heart. In essence, it is a place within oneself where one remembers to incline ones ears toward God and contemplate the contact of love between God and oneself. One might dare to say that the poustinia is the place where we make love. This loving contact can be made anywhere, even in the midst of a city, so long as the place is safe for us. A poustinia might be a conservation area or a public park full of benches and walking paths. It might be a cabin in the woods that we rent from time to time."XXXIV

See: Doherty, Catherine De Hueck. *Poustinia: Encountering God in Silence, Solitude and Prayer (Madonna House Classics)*. 3rd ed. Combermere, Ontario: Madonna House Pubns, 2000.

OUT-OF-PLACE ARTIFACTS

In pseudoarcheology the term "out-of-place artifact" refers to an object that exists in a place that it logically cannot belong due to distance and/or time. A fine example of such an object would be to find an iPod among the sand-buried ruins of Ancient Egypt.

Obviously such a discovery would fundamentally change the way in which people look at history and time, but of course no such revolutionary discovery has been made. Nevertheless there are several objects that certain people on the fringes of amateur research have claimed to exist that are completely out of place for the context in which they were found.

Perhaps the most complex and fascinating object was an analog computer orrery from the first or second-century BC discovered in 1900 among the ruins of a Roman shipwreck off the Greek island of Antikythera.

Ever since its discovery scientists have been attempting to decipher its gears and reconstruct the device, and many believe it is the oldest computer in the world, whose complexity rivals that of eighteenth-century Swiss clocks. *The Guardian* newspaper wrote:

"Detailed imaging of the mechanism suggests it dates back to 150-100 BC and had 37 gear wheels enabling it to follow the movements of the moon and the sun through the zodiac, predict eclipses and even recreate the irregular orbit of the moon. The motion, known as the first lunar anomaly, was developed by the astronomer Hipparcus of Rhodes in the 2nd century BC, and he may have been consulted in the machine's construction, the scientists speculate. . . .One of the remaining mysteries is why the Greek technology invented for the machine seemed to disappear. No other civilisation is believed to have created anything as complex for another 1,000 years."[xxxv]

The Tecaxic-Calixtlahuaca head, which is a terracotta sculpture of a head, was discovered in 1933 in a pre-Columbian grave in the Calixtlahuaca archeological site in Toluca outside of Mexico City. The head figure appears to be of Roman origin yet it was found located in a gravesite dating to the time period before contact between Europe and America. Most established archeologists and historians have agreed that the figurine is indeed of Roman origin and dates somewhere between the ninth and thirteenth-century AD. Romeo H. Hristov of the University of New Mexico and Santiago Genovese of the National Autonomous University of Mexico both state that "it is without any doubt Roman, and the lab analysis has confirmed that is ancient."[XXXVI]

Some argue that seemingly obvious man-made sculptures and designs stand completely out of their historical context, for example the Iron Pillar of Delhi. The pillar is 22-feet high, weighs over six tons, and made up of over 98-percent pure wrought iron. Due to the pillar's advanced metallic composition some argue that, much like the Antikythera mechanism is too advanced for being created in the fourth-century AD.

CARTHUSIAN AND CISTERCIAN ORDERS

In 1084 St. Bruno of Cologne founded the Roman Catholic religious order of the Carthusians, which is also known as the Carthusian Order.

The order is completely removed from the outside world, and is perhaps the most extreme form of Christian monasticism in the world today in that it requires its monks and nuns to live their lives in extreme physical and social isolation, some may say a voluntary solitary confinement.

As all Catholic monks the Carthusians observe the Liturgy of the Hours, but unlike other monastic orders the Carthusians observe the liturgy on their own in their private cells. [41]

Each cell is furnished with a bed, a table, and a kneeler for prayer. The cells have an exit into the main corridor of the monastery as well as an exit into the small private garden of the monk or nun where he or she can meditate and work on a garden. Food is delivered through a turnstile so that the monastics do not have to communicate or see the deliverer.

For most of the day the enclosed monastics live alone in silence, leaving the cell only three times per day for religious services in the chapel; once a week they take a community stroll through the monastery or countryside; on Sundays and

---

[41] The Liturgy of the Hours, also known as Divine Office, is a set of daily prayers at fixed hours in the Roman Catholic Church. A similar set of daily prayers is found in many Christian religions and goes back to pre-Christian Judaic tradition. The Divine Office is in essence the believer's daily duty before God. In Catholicism the prayers in the Divine Office are recited from the Breviary, a liturgical book of the Latin liturgical rites consisting of prayers, psalms, and hymns. The daily liturgical cycle begins with Vespers at sunset. It is followed by Compline, a meditation before sleep; then a Midnight Office is held at midnight; Matins is performed before dawn with the rising sun; then the Prime (First Hour) at seven in the morning, the Terce (Third Hour) at nine, the Sext (Sixth Hour) at noon, and the None (Ninth Hour) at three in the evening. For more information see *The Liturgy of the Hours.* Totowa: Catholic Book Publishing Company, 2005.

feast days they hold a community meal in silence; twice a year monks enjoy a full day of recreation, where they may speak and receive visitors.

The Cistercian monks and nuns are similar for they too are enclosed monastics, and the Trappists, a branch of the Cistercian order, are famous for their strict observance of the Rule of St. Benedict, as well as being exceptionally silent and speaking only when it is necessary, including during meal times. It is a common misconception that the Trappists take a so-called "vow-of-silence," however this is not the case for no such vow exists.

See: *The Carthusian Life*. Brookline: Charterhouse Of The Transfiguration, 2003.

MOUNT ATHOS

Located on the southern tip of one of the three peninsulas of Khalkidhiki in northeast Greece, Mount Athos – or "Holy Mountain" – is the home to a small community of monks with about twenty monasteries of the Order of St. Basil of the Orthodox Eastern Church.

The oldest monastery dates back to 963 AD. Mount Athos has remained rather independent from Greece and other nations to this day. In 1927 it became a theocratic republic ruled by the patriarch of Constantinople while under the suzerainty of Greece.

Graham Speke, who authored a book on the Holy Mountain, and converted to Orthodoxy, wrote about the preparation for visiting Athos:

"A visit to Mount Athos requires careful preparation. The pilgrim – and every visitor is by definition a pilgrim – must prepare himself not only materially and physically but also intellectually and spiritually. For the journey he is about to make is no ordinary pilgrimage, no mere passage through time and space, but a journey to another world. He must prepare himself to leave this world and to enter a world where every stone breathes prayers, a world where he will experience a foretaste of paradise, a world known to its inhabitants as the Garden of the Mother of God."[XXXVII]

No women or female animals are allowed into the religious territories, and Orthodox Christians take precedence over non-Orthodox Christians in issuances of permits to enter the territory. As of 2001 there were 2,262 inhabitants of the community comprised mostly of monks and unarmed religious guards. This has caused some controversy and frustration amongst certain groups.

See: Speake, Graham. *Mount Athos: renewal in paradise*. New Haven: Yale University Press, 2002.

RAËLISM

Raëlism was founded by Claude Vorilhon in 1974 by a twenty-eight year old former race car driver, singer-songwriter, and editor of the magazine *Auto Pop.* His inspiration for creating the religion came from a supposed contact with an extraterrestrial near the crater of an extinct volcano in Auvergne, France, when, as Arthur Goldwag has described in his *Cults, Conspiracies, and Secret Societies*, "a four-foot-tall, green-skinned entity with long dark hair emerged from a silver UFO and entrusted him with a message: that human beings were created in alien laboratories some twenty-five thousand years ago and planted on earth."[XXXVIII]

The movement's belief is centered on the concept that life on planet Earth was created by extraterrestrials called the Elohim. The movement argues that angels, gods, demons, and prophets have been mistaken by mankind, and were in fact extraterrestrials visiting humans and imparting knowledge. Besides these basic views, the Raëlians hold an extremely open view of human sexuality, arguing for sexual self-determination and so-called "sensual meditation." They believe that democracy should be replaced with Geniocracy (that only people whose intellectual capacity is 50 percent above average should rule the world), the abolition of private property, strict population control, and the establishment of a one world government.

Critics of the movement have argued that of all the described beliefs the group focuses most heavily on decadent behavior and provides a structured atmosphere where no-guilt hedonism and sexual experimentation is encouraged. *Salon* writer Taras Grescoe attended a Raël convention in Montreal, Canada, and observed that there was a disproportional amount of body-builders and belly dancers in attendance.[xxxix]

Though the group claims that it is a religion, the National Assembly of France deemed it a cult in 1995 and a similar condemnation came from the Belgian Chamber of Representatives in 1997. The group is also controversial because of its alleged dabbling with human cloning in the late 1990s and its use of the swastika.[42]

See: Goldwag, Arthur. *Cults, conspiracies, and secret societies: the straight scoop on Freemasons, the Illuminati, Skull and Bones, Black Helicopters, the New World Order, and many, many more.* New York: Vintage Books, 2009.

---

[42] Clonaid, a human cloning company with close ties to Raëlism, was founded in 1997. And in 2002 Brigitte Boisselier, its CEO, had claimed that they had cloned a baby girl, Eve.

THE DYATLOV PASS INCIDENT

On the night of February 1-2 1959 a strange and most terrifying event took place in the freezing hills of wild Siberia to a team of Soviet skiers.

Whatever occurred that night was so terrifying that it forced the highly experienced skiers to flee from their tents, half-naked, into the sub-zero tundra.[43]

By morning they were all dead.

There were ten people in all: Igor Dyatlov, 23, the leader of the group. Georgy Krivonishcenko, 24. Yuri Doroshenko, 21. Zinaida Kolmogorova, 22. Rustem Slobodin, 23. Nicolas Thibeaux-Brignollel, 24. Lyudmila Dubnina, 21. Alexander Zolotarev, 37. Alexander Kolevatov, 25, and Yuri Yudin, 22.

All of the skiers were highly skilled, and the younger ones were all students at elite universities throughout the Soviet Union.

The tragic story began on January 25, 1959 when the group travelled by train to the Sverdlovsk Oblast city of Ivdel'. The following day the group hitched a truck ride to the town of Vizhay, where they spent the night. On the 28th Yury Yudin became sick and decided to head back while the rest of the group began to trek along the river towards the hill known as Gora Otorten.

---

[43] According to some sources it was 5 degree Fahrenheit.

By the 31st the group reached the highland zone, breaking off from the river where they spent the day preparing for the uphill venture to Kholat Syakhl. Kholat Syakhl a hill which in the native Mansi language means "The Mountain of the Dead."

According to Mansi folklore the mountain is sacred and the area was once used as a place for mysticism and sorcery. On the morning of February 1 the Dyatlov group set off for the legendary hill and arrived at the slopes of the mountain where they set up camp by evening.

According to their personal notes they had all eaten a meal between 6 and 7. Between 7 and 10 the group settled down into their tents, some of them changed into their sleeping garments, suggesting that even though it was incredibly cold, -17C, some felt comfortable enough to change.

Most researchers agree that the mysterious and terrifying incident which resulted in the deaths of all the members of the expedition took place around 9:30 and 11:30 at night, when they had all retired to their tents.

The timeline and the events were later reconstructed by researchers and detectives based on the undigested food in their stomachs, the locations of their bodies, and evidence uncovered at the scene.

Sometime between 9:30 and 10:30 members of the expedition – some dressed in their hiking apparel and others only in their sleeping garments – cut through the sides of their tents and fled downhill from their campsite into the nearest forest.

The fact that they chose to cut through the tents instead of opening them and did not put on their clothing suggests that they were fleeing from something inevitable, and the fact that they were experienced hikers and understood that they would not survive long in the frigid temperatures suggests that whatever was occurring at the campsite was far more unsettling then certain hypothermic death.

According to the tracks found at the scene the group apparently was at first scattered into the forest, but later managed to come together as a group around 10:30.

For a about thirty minutes the group huddled or hid under a large pine tree a little over a mile from their campsite, swapping clothing with each other in order to stay warm.

It is estimated that at this point the group was already suffering from fatally frigid conditions and therefore decided to build a small fire. Apparently attempting to see what is happening at the campsite a member of the group climbed a pine tree – but later researchers would discover that the campsite was never visible from the tree. Forensic specialists would find traces of human flesh on the bark and top branches of that tree, which explained why the hands of some of the skiers were lacerated raw.

On the edge of death, disoriented and hopeless, Igor Dyatlov, Zinaida Kolmogorova, and Rustem Slobodin decided to make the trek back to their campsite, but none of them made it. Each collapsed and died at various intervals, Zinaida was the only member to come the closest back to the campsite.

While the three members were gone Georgy Krivonischenko and Yuri Doroshenko died from the cold. Some have suggested that their deaths may have occurred before Dyatlov, Kolmogorova and Slobodin left, and perhaps their deaths were the catalyst for the three to make the seemingly impossible trek back to the campsite.

The remaining members of the group took the clothes off all their deceased comrades and moved further away from the campsite deeper into the forest.

They eventually made it to a ravine where they huddled to stay warm. At that point Nicolas Thibeaux-Brignollel died from hypothermia, and later Lyudmila Dubnina died of hypothermia and chest injuries. Some have suggested the chest injuries were the result of running through the forest and bumping into trees and rocks or from falling into the ravine, which was also full of rocks.

After Dubnina died Alexander Zolotarev took her coat and hat in an attempt to stay warm. However he soon died from a combination of chest injuries and hypothermia. Between 1:30 and 2:45 in the morning the last member of the expedition, Alexander Kolevatov fell asleep and died.

The group was set to arrive in the town of Vishay on the 12th or 14th of February and send a telegram to the competition announcing their arrival. When no telegram had arrived by the 20th the parents and friends of the group began to urge their university and local authorities to become involved. On the 21st the Soviet military launched a search party for the skiers which also included a civilian search party.

The campsite and the bodies were discovered on February 26th and an official Soviet investigation was launched. The Soviet authorities could not find the reason for the skiers' sudden departure from their tents, only being able to conclude the reasons for the deaths, such as severe injuries, broken ribs, and most importantly hypothermia.

The only reasoning the official investigation came up with was that there was some sort of "compelling force" which compelled the experienced hikers to abandon their camp into certain death.

Several theories have been posited as a result of the mysterious nature of the incident, which has come to be known as the Dyatlov Pass Incident. One of these theories is that the group escaped an incoming avalanche, or the fear of one. Some have proposed that the high winds and strange sounds of the mountain at night may have driven the hikers into a state of panic and anxiety, that perhaps one or several of the hikers had escalated the panic by screaming "Avalanche!"

It has been observed that the Soviet air force was carrying out drills near the area, and another ski team some miles away noticed large orange lights in the sky and bizarre roars that may have been the test-flights of the MiG-21. The roar of the planes may have created the impression of snow and rocks hurtling down the hill towards the camp.

Others have proposed theories such as UFO's haunting and torturing the skiers, secret government experiments, and a theory that the local Mansi people were responsible for the tragedy. The Dyatlov Pass Incident remains a mystery. [44]

See: *"Dyatlov Pass Accident - The Mystery Begins."*
. *<http://www.aquiziam.com/dyatlov_pass_1.html>.*

---

[44] The route which the Dyatlov group took to the Mountain of the Dead has been renamed the Dyatlov Pass and a memorial plaque has been installed there.

ENDNOTES

I Gulik, Robert Hans van. *Sexual life in ancient China; a preliminary survey of Chinese sex and society from ca. 1500 B. C. till 1644 A. D..* Leiden: BRILL, 1961. 151.

II Behnke, Alison. *Niger in pictures .* Minneapolis, MN: Twenty-First Century Books, 2008. 15

III "L'Arbre du Ténéré, Part 2." *Jim Mann Taylor's Web Pages for The 153 Club (The Sahara Desert); and the NCCPG (Plant Conservation).* N.p., n.d. Web. 12 Dec. 2010. <http://www.manntaylor.com/tenere2.html>.

IV Manekin, Michael. "Body found in wheel well of Boeing 747 jet at SFO - Inside Bay Area." *Home - Inside Bay Area.* N.p., n.d. Web. 12 Dec. 2010. <http://www.insidebayarea.com/oaklandtribune/ci_6421583>.

V Miller, James Nevin. "The Passing of the Carrier Pigeon." *Popular Mechanics* Feb. 1930: 195

VI United States National Research Council, Economic Impacts of Severe Space Weather. "Severe space weather events ... - Google Books." *Google Books.* N.p., n.d. Web. 12 Apr. 2011. <http://books.google.com/books?id=RLi3G4P7fiIC&pg=PT44&dq=carrington+event&hl=en&ei=3dujTeCHHKnE0QGzgvD3CA&sa=X&oi=book_result&ct=result&resnum=1&ved=0CCgQ6AEwAA#v=onepage&q=carrington%20event&f=false>.

VII Sanders, Henry A. "The Number of the Beast in Revelation." *Journal of Biblical Literature* 37.1/2 (1918): 95-99.

VIII "Dakhma Summary | BookRags.com." *BookRags.com | Study Guides, Lesson Plans, Book Summaries and more.* N.p., n.d. Web. 13 Dec. 2010. <http://www.bookrags.com/research/dakhma-eorl-04/>

IX Clarke, Nicholas. *Black sun: Aryan cults, Esoteric Nazism, and the politics of identity.* New York: New York University Press, 2002. 116.

X Pomerantsev. "Appeals for Sincerity in the Writer." Current Digest of the Post-Soviet Press, 6 (March 24, 1954): 3-22.

XI Brown, Edward James. *Russian Literature since the Revolution.* Rev. and enl. ed. Cambridge, Mass.: Harvard University Press, 1982. 193-95

XII Schmelz, Peter John. *Such Freedom, If Only Musical : Unofficial Soviet Music During the Thaw.* Oxford ; New York: Oxford University Press, 2009. 6

XIII Barker, Adele Marie. Consuming Russia: popular culture, sex, and society since Gorbachev. Durham, N.C.: Duke University Press, 1999. 83

XIV See Соколова, Инна . *Авторская песня: от фольклора к поэзии.* Moscow: GKTsM V.S. Vysotskogo, 2002.

XV Taubman, William. *Khrushchev : The Man and His Era.* 1st ed. New York: Norton, 2003. 590

XVI Smith, Gerald Stanton. *Songs to Seven Strings : Russian Guitar Poetry and Soviet "Mass Song"*. Soviet History, Politics, Society, and Thought. Bloomington: Indiana University Press, 1984. 95

XVII Daughtry, J. Martin. "The Intonation of Intimacy: Ethics, Emotion, Metaphor, and Dialogue among Contemporary Russian Bards." Diss. University of California, Los Angeles. 2009. 183

XVIII Puckle, Bertram S.. *Funeral Customs: Their Origin and Development.* New edition ed. Detroit: Omnigraphics, 1990. 46–47.

XIX Pratt, Sara. "Lamont-Doherty Earth Observatory News." *Lamont-Doherty Earth Observatory* | . N.p., n.d. Web. 15 Dec. 2010. <http://www.ldeo.columbia.edu/news/2005/11_28_05.htm>.

XX Favazza, Armando R.. *Bodies under Siege: Self-mutilation and Body Modification in Culture and Psychiatry.* second edition ed. Baltimore: The Johns Hopkins University Press, 1996: 38-39.

XXI Gibbon, Edward. *The history of the decline fall of the roman empire* . London: Henry Frowde, 1967. 1022

XXII "Baphomet Facts, information, pictures | Encyclopedia.com articles about Baphomet." Encyclopedia - Online Dictionary | Encyclopedia.com: Get facts, articles, pictures, video. N.p., n.d. Web. 9 Apr. 2011. <http://www.encyclopedia.com/topic/Baphomet.asp>.

XXIII Stager, Lawrence. "Why Were Hundreds of Dogs Buried at Ashkelon? - Biblical Archaeology Review." *Bible History & Archaeology Published by the Biblical Archaeology Society | Biblical Archaeology Review* . N.p., n.d. Web. 15 Dec. 2010. <http://www.bib-arch.org/e-features/dogs-buried-at-ashkelon.asp#location1>.

XXIV Zielenziger, Michael. *Shutting out the sun: how Japan created its own lost generation.* New York: Nan A. Talese, 2006. 2.

XXV Bondeson, Jan. Buried alive: the terrifying history of our most primal fear. New York: Norton, 2001. 221

XXVI Funck-Brentano, Frantz. "The Man with the Iron Mask." *The Chautauquan* Feb. 1895: 531.

XXVII *Ibid, 532.*

XXVIII Dokoupil, Tony. "William Powell Expresses Regret About His Anarchist Cookbook - The Daily Beast ." *The Daily Beast.* N.p., n.d. Web. 9 Apr. 2011. <http://www.thedailybeast.com/blogs-and-stories/2011-02-22/william-powell-expresses-regret-about-his-anarchist-cookbook/#>.

XXIX "Amazon.com: The Anarchist Cookbook (9780962303203): William Powell, Peter Bergman: Books." *Amazon.com: Online Shopping for Electronics, Apparel, Computers, Books, DVDs & more.* N.p., n.d. Web. 9 Apr. 2011. <http://www.amazon.com/Anarchist-Cookbook-William-Powell/dp/0962303208>.

XXX "Dowsing Facts, information, pictures | Encyclopedia.com articles about Dowsing." *Encyclopedia - Online Dictionary | Encyclopedia.com: Get facts, articles, pictures, video.* N.p., n.d. Web. 9 Apr. 2011. <http://www.encyclopedia.com/topic/Dowsing.aspx#2-1G2:3406300160-full>.

XXXI Robson, Michael. *St. Francis of Assisi: the Legend and the Life.* London: Continuum, 1999. 263.

XXXII Elgin, Suzette Haden. "Láadan, the Constructed Language in Native Tongue, by Suzette Haden Elgin." *SFWA* . N.p., n.d. Web. 25 Dec. 2010. <http://www.sfwa.org/members/elgin/Laadan.html>.

XXXIII Gurmukh, Kaur Khalsa. *Kundalini Rising: Exploring the Energy of Awakening.* Boulder, CO: Sounds True, 2009. 4–5.

XXXIV Stairs, Jean. *Listening for the Soul: Pastoral Care and Spiritual Direction.* Minneapolis: Fortress, 2000. 67.

XXXV "Mysteries of computer from 65BC are solved | Science | The Guardian ." *Latest news, comment and reviews from the Guardian | guardian.co.uk* . N.p., n.d. Web. 29 Apr. 2011. <http://www.guardian.co.uk/scie nce/2006/nov/30/uknews>.

XXXVI "Calixtlahuaca's Head." *The University of New Mexico.* N.p., n.d. Web. 29 Apr. 2011. <http://www.unm.edu/~rhristov/calixtlahuaca.html>.

XXXVII Speake, Graham. *Mount Athos: renewal in paradise.* New Haven: Yale University Press, 2002. 17.

XXXVIII Goldwag, Arthur. *Cults, conspiracies, and secret societies: the straight scoop on Freemasons, the Illuminati, Skull and Bones, Black Helicopters, the New World Order, and many, many more.* New York: Vintage Books, 2009. 91.

XXXIX Grescoe, Taras. "Raël love - Canada - Salon.com." *Salon.com - Salon.com.* N.p., n.d. Web. 30 Apr. 2011. <http://www.salon.com/travel/feature/2000/03/08/raelians/>.

ABOUT SASHA POGREBINSKY

Sasha holds an M.A. in Russian Studies from New York University and is fluent in Russian, Ukrainian, and English.
Sasha owns Bear, a bar and restaurant in New York City.
More information on the author is available at:
www.pogrebinsky.info